The Minimum Core for

Language and Literacy:

Audit and Test

Lynn Machin

LearningMatters

First published in 2009 by Learning Matters Ltd

British Library Cataloguing in Publication Data
A CIP record for this book is available from the British Library.

ISBN 978 1 84445 271 2

Cover design by Topics – The Creative Partnership
Project Management by Deer Park Productions, Tavistock, Devon
Typeset by Pantek Arts Ltd, Maidstone, Kent
Printed and bound in Great Britain by Bell & Bain Ltd, Glasgow

Learning Matters Ltd
33 Southernhay East
Exeter EX1 1NX
Tel: 01392 215560
info@learningmatters.co.uk
www.learningmatters.co.uk

Mixed Sources
Product group from well-managed
forests and other controlled sources
www.fsc.org   Cert no. TT-COC-002769
© 1996 Forest Stewardship Council

FSC

📞 01603 773114
email: tis@ccn.ac.uk 🐦 @CCN_Library Ⓦ ccnlibraryblog.wordpress.com
f /ccninformationstore

21 DAY LOAN ITEM

Please return <u>on or before</u> the last date stamped above

A fine will be charged for overdue items

CITY COLLEGE NORWICH

Contents

The author vii

Acknowledgements ix

Introduction 1

Self-audit – personal language skills, literacy 5

1 Communication 7

2 Reading 17

3 Writing conventions 27

4 Punctuation 43

5 Spelling 56

6 Speaking and listening 65

Extracts from Minimum Core Framework 77

Answers to key questions 83

Glossary of terms 91

Index 93

The author

Lynn Machin

Lynn Machin is Award Leader and Senior Lecturer at Staffordshire University within the School of Education. She has over 20 years' experience of teaching in post-14 education. Lynn has had a variety of roles within ITT, including Award Leader, Curriculum Leader and Study Skills tutor. She has been part of a writing team for modules for the PTLLS, CTLLS and DTLLS programme within the University.

Acknowledgements

To my husband and children.
To all who read this book – enjoy learning and best wishes with your studies.

Every effort has been made to trace the copyright holders and to obtain their permission for the use of copyright material. The publisher and author will gladly receive any information enabling them to rectify any error or omission in subsequent editions.

Introduction

Why do trainee teachers need to meet the Minimum Core requirements?

Background

The Lifelong Learning Sector (LLS) has a very varied work force and offers a wide range of academic, vocational and recreational programmes of learning for learners aged from 14 upwards.

Teachers join the LLS, generally known as further education (FE), from various backgrounds (i.e. industry, professional practices, university or college, home workers, unemployment or redundancy).

What all these teachers have in common is expertise in subjects that are suitable for delivery within a Further Education college or a training organisation. These subjects have an extensive range, for example gardening, walking, tai chi, hairdressing, computing, work-based learning and traditional GCSE and A level subjects. All fall into one of three categories: academic, vocational or recreational. Historically, teachers within FE did not need to have a teaching qualification or need to demonstrate competence within the Minimum Core requirements.

However, superseding the implementation, in 2001, of the Further Education National Training Organisation (FENTO) standards, the Lifelong Learning UK (LLUK) standards were introduced in 2007. The legislation driving these standards made it a mandatory requirement for teachers working within the Lifelong Learning sector to be qualified and to have a Licence to Practise.

Qualified status can be sought through the Associate Teacher route (for those teachers not engaged in a full teaching role) or through the Diploma route (for those teachers engaged in a full teaching role). Moreover, for the first time the Lifelong Learning Sector has its own professional body, namely the Institute for Learning (IfL). All teachers within the Lifelong Learning Sector have to register with the IfL and provide evidence of at least 30 hours a year continuing professional development (CPD). Following the completion and accreditation of an LLUK qualification the first year of a teacher's CPD is for Professional Formation following which either Associate Teacher Learning and Skills (ATLS) status or Qualified Teacher Learning and Skills (QTLS) status is awarded to them.

What is the Minimum Core?

The minimum core was founded in 2004 to support Awarding Bodies and Initial Teacher Training (ITT) providers to equip ITTs with the skills necessary to develop inclusive approaches to teaching and learning. The revised Minimum Core (2007) includes, for the first time, information communication technology (ICT).

The Minimum Core is the minimum level that teachers should be operating at in the core subjects of language, literacy, numeracy and ICT (i.e. all teachers should be operating within these core subjects at a minimum of level two). This level two requirement corresponds to level two within the National Qualification Framework.

There is a list of references at the end of this book, including one relating to the National Qualification Framework. Information should also be available through colleges and training organisations. Level two is equivalent to GCSE grades A–C or equivalent qualifications.

The language and literacy component of the Minimum Core includes:

- speaking, listening and responding;
- reading and comprehending;
- writing as a means to communicate.

Professional Formation and the Minimum Core – evidencing personal skills in literacy

The Minimum Core is based upon subject specialism (literacy, language, numeracy, ICT) with no notion of ITT professionalisation within it. However, embedded within the LLUK (2007) standards, and also within the IfL's Professional Formation process, is the concept of the Minimum Core and how the skills defined within it may be contextualised within teaching practice.

Operating at level two ensures that teachers are fully prepared for their role as a professional teacher. It provides a platform for teachers and ITTs to develop these essential skills further. Under the IfL's (2007) regulations (number 2264) it is stated that: *no person may be employed in a teaching role unless that person has completed such a programme to the satisfaction of IfL, or has obtained such award as may be deemed approved by the Secretary of State, for the purposes of demonstrating that a person has the necessary literacy, numeracy and information and communications technology skills to teach.* (DIUS, IfL, LLUK, SVUK, 2007, page 1).

The IfL recognises that some people will have already attained competence in literacy, language, numeracy or ICT and evidence (e.g. scanned certificates) can be submitted to the IfL as evidence of attainment.

Moreover, the IfL (2007), with collaboration from LLUK, has stated that teachers have five years to achieve this Professional Formation from when they commence their pro-gramme of study, whether this programme of study is for Associate Teacher Learning and Skills (ATLS) or Qualified Teacher Learning and Skills (QTLS) status.

Essentially, Professional Formation is a teacher's conferral as a professional qualified and licensed practitioner.

Mandatory LLUK units where evidence of working towards/at/above the Minimum Core is required

Within the LLUK (2007) qualification framework the Minimum Core is covered in the fol-lowing units:

- Planning and enabling learning (within CTLLS and DTLLS);
- Enabling learning and assessment (DTLLS);
- Theories and principles for planning and enabling learning (DTLLS).

The Minimum Core Personal Skills (literacy skills are covered within this book) must be included in each of the three units listed above. Knowledge and understanding should be linked to the three units as appropriate and target-setting should be scheduled to enable trainees to develop their knowledge, understanding and skills. Other LLUK units, including the option units, could include evidence of the Minimum Core depending upon the requirements of the Awarding Body.

Why are teachers and ITT trainees being asked to evidence the Minimum Core before they can attain Professional Formation?

A question asked by many ITT trainees of their teachers is why they have to demonstrate competence within language, literacy, numeracy and ICT when they have no intention of teaching these subjects and their subject does not specifically include or embed these Minimum Core topics. Some ITT trainees comment that because they teach adults and not 14–19 year olds they are not required to teach functional skills. A further comment is that they (the trainees) are not English, mathematics or ICT teachers. The answer to these comments is three-fold.

First, when planning for teaching and learning, teachers need to be equipped with at least the level two Minimum Core skills to enable them to embed functional skills (language, literacy, numeracy and ICT) in teaching and learning that are appropriate for their learners. OFSTED promotes, through its inspection framework, the embedding of functional skills for all learners and likewise this practice will probably be promoted by colleges and training organisations. Methods of embedding literacy into teaching and learning could include:

- providing feedback in relation to grammar, spelling and punctuation to learners following the marking of their work;
- giving learners presentations, reports, notices and other work that requires them to demonstrate their language and literacy skills while engaged in their subject specialism.

Second, specifically with literacy and language, a teacher's competence in literacy and language (verbal communication, preparation of handouts, etc.) will impact upon the learners' levels of literacy and language through naturally occurring and planned activities and through the hidden curriculum (that which occurs within the classroom but is unplanned). It is, as commented upon by LLUK (2007) in relation to trainees gaining competence at (or above) the Minimum Core level, imperative that teachers are able to fully support learner achievement.

Third, some learners have left school with poor literacy and language skills but do not want to attend a course that specifically addresses the deficit in these skills. Some learners may benefit from enrolling on a course that they are interested in and which also provides opportunities to develop literacy and language skills within an embedded context. If learners can improve upon their literacy and language skills, then they can improve their opportunities for employment and also raise their self-esteem and confidence. Teachers therefore need to be able to plan sessions that promote and encourage improvement and consolidation of literacy and language skills.

From a personal perspective some ITT trainees and teachers worry about writing on the board in front of their learners because of poor handwriting and spelling. They may also miss opportunities to correct learners' written work appropriately because of their own lack of understanding in relation to grammar, spelling and punctuation use. Good communication, literacy and language skills are constantly required, for example:

- attending open evenings;
- giving presentations;
- performing everyday administration tasks;
- preparing for inspections;
- submitting reports to line managers;
- teaching;
- writing reports to parents or guardians.

To be seen as professional, teachers need to be competent within their subject area (a subject specialist) and to be competent as a teacher (an education specialist), which includes meeting the Minimum Core level two requirements. Therefore, operating at the Minimum Core is something that every teacher should want to do for their own personal development and for the well-being of their learners.

About this book

This book comprises skills-building exercises to enable you to meet the requirements laid down in the Minimum Core (2007) guidance document, namely:

> *Addressing literacy, language, numeracy and ICT needs in education and training: Defining the minimum core of teachers' knowledge, understanding and personal skills. A guide for initial teacher education programmes.*

The chapters within this book contribute towards the:

- Minimum Core Personal Skills
- LLUK Professional Standards (A–F)

Extracts from the Minimum Core framework that relate to the development of personal skills in literacy and language can be found towards the end of this book.

Objectives are also linked to the Adult Literacy Core Curriculum.

REFERENCES AND FURTHER READING REFERENCES AND FURTHER READING

The references below are taken from the *Minimum Core Handbook* (2007):
Department for Education and Skills (2001) Adult Literacy Core Curriculum. London: DfES.
Department for Education and Skills (2001) Adult ESOL Core Curriculum. London: DfES.
Department for Education and Skills (2001) Pre-Entry Curriculum Framework. London: DfES.
Department for Education and Skills (2001) Access for All. London: DfES.
Department for Education and Skills (2002) Introducing Access for All. London: DfES.
Qualifications and Curriculum Authority (2000) National Basic Skills Standards. London: QCA.
Qualifications and Curriculum Authority (2004) Communication Key Skill. London: QCA.

Websites
The Adult Literacy Core Curriculum (2008, pages 126–31): **www.dfes.gov.uk/ curriculum_literacy/tree/writing/writingcomp/l2/**
The Institute for Learning: **www.ifl.ac.uk/services/p_wwv_page?id=140**
The LLUK (2007) Standards: **www.lluk.org.uk**
LLUK (Sept., 2008) Evidencing Personal Skills in Literacy and Numeracy, Guidance to Teachers and Employers: **www.lluk.org/documents/evidencing-personal-skills-requirements.pdf**
The Minimum Core (2007) Framework: **www.lluk.org/documents/minimum_core_may _2007_3rd.pdf**
National Qualification Framework: **www.direct.gov.uk/en/EducationAndLearning/ QualificationsExplained/DG_**
Standards Verification UK: **www.standardsverificationuk.org/documents/ Evidencing_the_personal_skills_in_English_Mathematics_and_ICT_FINAL.pdf**

Self-audit – personal language skills, literacy

The following audit will help you to identify and to reflect upon your current skill level. You may find it useful to discuss your answers with a friend, colleague or ITT teacher.

Be as honest as you can be when completing the table below.

Consider the following competence-related statements and award yourself a mark out of five. Five is the highest and one is the lowest mark that you can award yourself. Can you think of examples and evidence to support your judgement of the mark awarded? If necessary, consider what action you could take to improve your skills (e.g. doing the exercises within this book and seeking guidance from your ITT teacher).

Speaking	1	2	3	4	5	Examples and/or evidence to support your judgement	Action
Express yourself clearly using communication techniques to help convey meaning and to enhance the delivery and accessibility of the message.							
Demonstrate the ability to use language, style and tone in ways that suit the intended audience, and recognise their use by others.							
Use appropriate techniques to reinforce oral communication and to check how well the information is received. Support the understanding of those listening.							
Use non-verbal communication to assist in conveying meaning and receive information, and recognise its use by others.							
Listening	1	2	3	4	5	**Examples and/or evidence to support your judgement**	**Action**
Listen attentively and respond sensitively to contributions made by others.							

Reading	1	2	3	4	5	Examples and/or evidence to support your judgement	Action
Find and select information from a range of reference material and sources of information, including the internet.							
Use and reflect on a range of reading strategies to interpret texts and to locate information or meaning.							
Identify and record the key information or messages contained within reading material using note-taking techniques.							
Writing	1	2	3	4	5	Examples and/or evidence to support your judgement	Action
Write fluently, accurately and legibly on a range of topics.							
Select appropriate format and style of writing for different purposes and different readers.							
Use spelling and punctuation accurately in order to make meaning clear.							
Understand and use the conventions of grammar consistently when producing written text.							

Source: Addressing Literacy, Language, Numeracy and ICT needs in education and training: defining the Minimum Core of Teachers' Knowledge, Understanding and Personal Skills. (LLUK, 2007, pp20–24)

The above exercise will have enabled you to reflect upon your current literacy skills and may have identified areas that you need to improve.

Once you have worked your way through the book and completed a range of exercises, complete the skills audit again.

1
Communication

By the end of this chapter you should be able to:

- reflect upon your current ability to communicate effectively;
- use a range of communication techniques with a range of people for different purposes;
- provide examples of non-verbal communication;
- appreciate reasons for considering appropriate meta-language;
- give reasons why confidentiality is important.

This chapter and its objectives contribute to the following Minimum Core requirements: Part B; Personal Language Skills: Speaking, Listening and Writing.

This chapter also contributes towards the following LLUK standards:
AS4, AS7, AP4.2, AP4.3, AK5.1, AK5.2, AP5.1, AP5.2, BS.3, BP3.1, BP3.4, BK3.4, CK3.3, CK3.4, CP3.3, CP3.4.
Also relevant to the Adult Core Curriculum S/R/W L2.

Communication is covered throughout many of the chapters in this book because writing, spelling, punctuation, listening and speaking all relate to communication. Discussed within this chapter are aspects of communication that enhance or underpin those topic areas covered in other chapters.

Key information

What is communication?

Communication is the way in which people relate to one another and also how information is passed on from person to person.

Communication can be categorised under three headings:

- *verbal* – this topic is covered in more depth in the chapter 'Speaking and listening';
- *written* – this topic is covered in more depth in the chapter 'Writing conventions';
- *non-verbal* communication (NVC).

Verbal communication is the message that we give, and receive, through the spoken use of language. NVC is the message that is given, and received, through the use of body language, for example, smiling, frowning, arms folded, tapping foot, leaning forward, playing with hair. Communication also includes all of the written messages that we provide, for example, letters, reports, forms, handouts, written presentations, email and text.

Why is communication important?

How you communicate with your learners, your line managers, colleagues and others that you come into contact with during your working day is extremely important. You need to ensure that the message or information you want to give is the information that is received. Furthermore people, including you, make decisions based upon messages and information received from others. You give an impression of yourself by what you say and the actions that you make. Most, if not all, people will judge you on how you communicate with them.

Importantly, if your communication skills are poor or in need of some development (written, verbal or non-verbal), then the learners' learning experience could be negatively affected.

Social learning, modelling and communication

Social learning and modelling refers to the behaviours that we acquire and develop as a result of the people we spend time with. Our dialect, accent, use of language and the body language we use is very much influenced by our parents, friends, peers and teachers.

Learners will, to differing extents, model their behaviour on their teachers, and that includes you. If you introduce them to new words they may begin to use them. The way you speak, the non-verbal actions you use and the written communication you use will all create a social learning experience for your learners. You need to ensure that it is a positive and enriching experience.

The English language, as with other languages, is continually changing and developing. Some words are no longer in existence and other words are gradually being introduced through various forms of media and different cultures. For example, new words are formed to describe new technologies and each generation of teenagers forms their own sub-culture of language.

Often we change the way we speak to suit the people we are with. We may alternate our language between formal and informal. For example, you may use a very formal and polite voice when speaking over the telephone and then perhaps when you are with your friends you may talk very quickly and informally. You may use slang and you will almost definitely use colloquialisms.

EXAMPLE

Examples of formal language:

- *Good afternoon, how may I help you?*
- *To whom am I speaking, please?*
- *I will endeavour to be of assistance to you and your partner.*
- *They do not do their homework; they just watch the television all night.*

Examples of informal language:

- *Hi, can I help?*
- *Who is it?*
- *I'll try to help you both, if I can.*
- *They don't do their homework; they are just couch potatoes.*

Can you think of any others that you use?

Cultural differences

In your personal and professional life you will meet people from different socio-economic and cultural backgrounds. It is important that you are aware that some verbal and non-verbal communication language (NVC) means different things to different people. These differences may matter a great deal because of the receiver's potential to misunderstand, misinterpret or even to feel insulted by the message. While you cannot always know what language and NVC signs your learners, and others that you meet with, find inappropriate or offensive, you can become observant of their body language and interpret their reaction to them.

How good are you at verbal and non-verbal communication?

Good verbal and non-verbal communication involves speaking clearly and using language appropriate to the audience. It also involves the use of NVC to support the verbal message; at times, non-verbal gestures are sufficient without any verbal message attached.

Facial expressions
NVC facial expressions include:

- smiling
- laughing
- frowning
- yawning
- blushing
- nodding

These are the most frequently used non-verbal body language. Eyes possibly express the most.

When you are speaking and listening, make sure that you look at the people with whom you are communicating. You will be able to judge their interest in what you are saying and also, when they are speaking, you will be able to judge if what they are saying is actually what they are thinking. While some people are very good at hiding their natural body language, most of us have not developed that skill and our body language can provide much information to those who are watching it.

As a teacher it is important that your facial expressions reflect what you are saying. For example, if you are praising a learner you would probably smile. Alternatively, if you were reprimanding a learner you would have a stern expression on your face. To give a learner a mixed message, for example to reprimand but be smiling, could confuse the learner or make them think that you do not really mean what you are saying.

Other facial expressions and gestures to note are:

- *scratching head* – when unsure about what is being said;
- *biting nails* – this can be a sign of anxiety;
- *winking* – indicates a joke, a playful attitude or empathy;
- *touching the chin* – indicates thinking;
- *face in hands* – indicates boredom.

Posture
If you slouch in class or look lethargic, your learners may think that you are not interested in teaching them. They may model your body language and be less interested in your teaching than if you were alert and standing upright. Your learners will mirror your language and that includes your body language.

The amount of space that you leave between yourself and other people you are communicating with is an indication of how well you know the person or people, how formal the communication is and also how comfortable you are with the person or people. Difference in upbringing also impacts upon how much space we like to have between us and others. As a teacher it is important that you demonstrate the right amount of spatial awareness between you and your learners. When you are teaching, try not to sit, or stand, behind the teacher's desk. This can be an indication of either fear (i.e. you need something between the pupils and you for protection), or it can be an indication of your lack of approachability. Do not be tactile with your learners; some learners might find even a small gesture of contact (touching shoulder or arm) offensive.

Appropriate language

As a teacher it is important that you recognise the appropriate use of meta-language. This means reflecting upon the language used by your learners and yourself. It also means discussing the language used if necessary to aid the learning process. You can do this by explaining or discussing any newly introduced words and importantly being mindful of socio-cultural differences.

If learners have ceased to be engaged in the class activities it is worth considering your communication skills. I once noticed one of my learners talking to the person next to her when she should have been listening to me. She was a very keen and good learner and always wanted to make sure that she had all of the information to take home with her for her assignments. I was therefore very surprised that she was not engaging in the lesson. I later discovered that it was because I had used the word 'tweaking' and the learner (because English was not her first language) did not know what this word meant and was worried that it was something really important, maybe even a point of theory – and that was what she was asking the person next to her about. The fault lay with me for introducing words, without explanation, which not all of my learners knew.

As with the example above, it is very important that your choice of language is suitable for your audience. If your learners have poor vocabulary skills you can introduce new words to them but explain briefly what the words mean.

It is also important that you use appropriate language when praising or speaking to learners. For example, if a learner asks you a question avoid saying *I've just told you that* or *haven't you been listening*? You will communicate a very negative message to the learners and they may become disengaged. An alternative way to approach this would be to ask the other learners if they know the answer.

HINTS AND TIPS

Whether you are writing or speaking, never mix up the following two words:

- fewer
- less

Use 'fewer' if you can count the numbers and 'less' if you cannot. 'Fewer' refers to plural (countable) items and 'less' refers to singular items (including collective nouns).

Examples of correct use:

- There are fewer chairs in the classroom than there were yesterday.
- There is less milk in the jug now.

Jargon

Jargon is the term used for 'in-house' or 'sub-culture' language. For example teachers talk about:

- Refec – Refectory/café
- SMT – Senior management team
- SAR – Self Assessment Report
- SED – Self Assessment Document

Teachers will also use technical jargon that relates to their specific subject. Others who are not familiar with the subject may not understand.

Teenagers use some words that some of us, as we get older, may have difficulty under-standing and these words, like teenagers' clothes or choice of music, change regularly. It is useful to understand teenage jargon, particularly if you teach this age range, but it is not necessary for you to use the jargon. These words belong to teenagers and the sub-culture that they live in.

Using jargon with other teachers or other people who understand the terminology is acceptable but avoid it, or explain it, if you are speaking with someone who may not understand it.

Being prepared to communicate

Good communication is a skill. It is a skill that seemingly comes more easily to some than others but is a skill that we all need to practise and to develop, particularly when we are working within education and we have a responsibility to communicate efficiently and effectively to our learners, line managers and others.

Being prepared, thinking about what you want to say or write, are essential ingredients for the development and maintenance of good communication skills.

HINTS AND TIPS
- The quality of any contribution that you make during meetings or other discussions is more important than the quantity of contributions that you make.
- Use positive language rather than negative language.

Listen carefully to other people's comments and make a note of any words that you are unsure of; this will improve your own word usage.

Always try to read appropriate information prior to meetings. This will give you an opportunity to consider any questions that you may want to ask.

You should always proofread handouts and presentations. Your learners will notice your mistakes, so try not to make any.

Ask if you do not understand something.

Think before you speak: words cannot be retracted and it is often very difficult to improve a relationship, even a professional one, if someone is upset by your words.

Communication errors
Joke books and circular emails often contain reference to communication errors. Some examples are:

- Toilet out of order. Please use floor below.
- After the tea break staff should empty the teapot and stand upside down on the draining board.
- On a Friday the teachers go off in the afternoon.

Although we can laugh at the above messages, our own messages should never be ambiguous. Read and if necessary re-read your work. If the message is important it is often a good idea to ask someone to read it first – what makes sense to you may not make sense to someone else. Read your work aloud if necessary; if it does not sound right it probably will not read right. Communication is not just about talking. Consider how much time you spend in your classroom speaking and listening. Listening is as important, if not more so, than speaking. How do you know that the learners have learned anything if you are not spending enough time listening to them?

Technology and media to improve communication

Information communication technology (ICT) has transformed the way that many people communicate. Email is arguably the most common technological mode of day-to-day communication. As a teacher you will probably have internal and external contacts all with email addresses. It is useful to use the distribution list function within the email set up. This function allows you to have lists of people's addresses that you can, at the touch of a button, send the same email to.

As well as emails there is now a range of virtual learning environments (VLEs) available. These VLEs have chat and discussion forums that can be set up between learners and you. VLEs are also useful for depositing presentations, video clips, lesson plans and other resources.

Within your teaching you will need to use a range of differing technologies to engage the learners and to assist you when planning teaching and learning methods that include visual, audio and kinaesthetic (VAK) modes of learning. The use of ICT forms part of the OFSTED framework and effective use of it is a consideration when grading observations.

Specialist software for delivering presentations is a medium that is now frequently used. When using this type of software remember the following points.

- Slides should support and enhance what you are saying.
- You should use a suitable size font to enable all learners to see the words clearly. As a minimum this should be 14 point, but often a font of 18 point plus is used.
- If you use images, ensure that they support your message.
- All words and images used must be socio-culturally inclusive.

When using specialist software for delivering presentations consider, if you do not already do it, embedding video clips or DVDs, many of which can be located from teacher training sites from the internet. The use of audio as well as visual presentation will provide opportunities for differentiation through teaching and learning strategies.

Other methods of communication through the use of ICT include the seemingly increasing use of digital cameras and the interactive whiteboard. The interactive whiteboard can be used by learners as well as teachers and what is written can be captured electronically, saved and used again at a later date.

No technology or media should be dismissed without thought about its usefulness to enhance teaching and learning. New and emerging technologies include audio visual equipment which can aid communication. Of course some technology will be too expensive or not appropriate within different teaching environments, but as a teacher you need to keep an open mind in relation to how technology can support communication and the learning process. For example, many teachers now have their learners' mobile telephone numbers and they also give their learners their mobile telephone number so that everyone is contactable. It is up to individual teachers and the regulations of the institution in which they work if they agree to this practice or not.

There is an increasing range of technology available for use by people with specific difficulties.

- *People who wear hearing aids* can use a loop system. Equipment that provides sub-titles may be available within your institution. Ask the learners what resources they are aware of and direct them to the learning support staff if necessary to enable equipment to be provided.
- *Partially sighted or blind people* can make use of computers with voice-activated software. When preparing resources for learners with visual impairment, use a large font and leave plenty of white space around the words. Leaving white space aids visibility and therefore aids the seeing and reading process.
- *Learners with dyslexia* often request that their resources are put onto coloured, rather than white, paper. Exactly which colour paper to produce handouts on is dependent upon the learner, but often the request is for cream or purple.

If you have learners in your class who have specific difficulties, approach the support networks within your institution and see what technology is available for them to improve their learning experience.

Consult the Information Technology (IT) technicians to see what is available within your institution. It is also a good idea to attend CPD sessions that relate to the use of new and emerging ICT. Embrace technology and consider what it can do for your learners and also for you.

Ethics and confidentiality

As a teacher you are a professional. You may still be undergoing training, and perhaps be considered as a trainee teacher, but you still need to act professionally at all times. This professionalism includes adhering to ethical and confidentiality parameters and legislation.

For example, learners may talk negatively about other teachers to you. They may support their comments by saying how much better you are than the other teachers. Do not ever be tempted to agree with them. If you do and at a later stage a learner complains about a teacher they may include a statement that you agreed with them about their view of the teacher.

Likewise do not give learners confidential information about other learners. This is more difficult than you might at first think. What may seem to you as a harmless question about someone may be seen by the person in question as a breach of confidentiality. For example:

Learner: 'It's strange Maureen is not in class today – is she ill?'
Teacher: 'Maureen has a hospital appointment today.'

It could be that Maureen wanted to keep her hospital appointment confidential and is so annoyed that you have told the learner (who has subsequently told the whole class) that she writes a letter of complaint to your Principal.

The above example might seem far fetched, particularly if you are new to teaching, but you should adopt the practice of never giving information away to other people without permission; unless, of course, it is to another professional who needs to have the information.

Data Protection Act (1998) and the Freedom of Information Act (2000)

The Data Protection Act (1998) allows people to request information from public bodies if the information is about them. The Act also legislates that information should not be kept by any public body unless it is currently necessary to do so.

The Freedom of Information Act (2000) allows people to request information from public bodies, although information deemed to be sensitive may not, even if requested, be given out.

Both of these Acts mean that anyone can ask to see any information that you have written about them. This includes emails as well as more formal records like learners' reports. Be careful about what information you provide – ensure that it is accurate and, if personal comments are necessary, make sure that you make them in a professional way and can, if necessary, provide evidence or examples to support your comments.

Never engage in gossip. First, if you do, you will soon become known as a gossip. Second, you could have the wrong information which could be detrimental to the person that you are gossiping about. Third, if you slander someone you could face a disciplinary hearing. When it comes to confidentiality, it is better to say less than more.

Key questions

Now have a go at the exercises below.
These exercises are designed to help you test yourself in this topic. Some are reflective questions and thus require you to discuss your potential answers with colleagues/tutors. Some require you to use a dictionary, spell checker or other resources that will be available to you. Work through the exercises and note your answers on a separate sheet. The answers can be found at the back of the book.

Q1 The following words might be used in informal speech or informal writing but how would you change them if you were being more formal? An example is provided.

    exam – examination
1. info –
2. demo –
3. phone –
4. a.s.a.p –
5. comp –
6. typo –

Q2 Read the following scenario and consider what message the teacher (Ms Mountford) may be communicating through use of NVC to her learners.

It is Friday afternoon and the teacher, Ms Mountford, is in her classroom with a group of learners aged 16–18. Ms Mountford keeps looking at her watch and often walks to the window to look outside. The learners are quite interested in the topic they have been set and are behaving well but begin to notice their teacher's behaviour. They ask a few questions about the topic and their teacher either answers or suggests that they ask someone else in the class. Eventually, the learners look at their watches and start to pack away their work and folders although it is ten minutes before the session ends. Ms Mountford sighs but does not say anything.

Q3 What do the following gestures mean?

1. thumbs up
2. thumbs down
3. thumping the air
4. walking briskly
5. clapping

Q4 Consider whether you should use written or verbal communication in the following situations:

1. To set the ground rules for a new group of learners.
2. To praise a learner.
3. To raise a concern over a learner to their parents.
4. To provide statistics in readiness for an OFSTED inspection.
5. To provide information about your learners' progress and achievement.
6. To provide a reference for a learner.

Q5 Fill in the missing words.

When considering ethics and .... it is important to remember the ...., Act and the .... of .... These two ..... are to protect the public and that includes your learners.

Q6 Watch a DVD or video with the sound turned down. Try to interpret what is happening by observing the performers' non-verbal communication. Replay the DVD or video and see if your observations were correct.

Q7 Using a dictionary, or glossary of terms if necessary, state what the following abbreviations mean:

BA, RSVP, MA, IfL, NVQ, NEET, BTEC, HE, PhD, WBL

Q8 Read the following transcript from a conversation between a teacher and the parents of Deborah, who is one of the teacher's pupils. Is there anything wrong with it and if so, how could it be improved?

Yea, Debbie's doin OK. She, em, got good marks in her mocks but she needs to use Moodle more for info about deadlines; she's not too hot on them. Deb's late for lessons sometimes because she spends too much time in the refec. Other than that I'd say that with a bit of effort she could get As and Bs in her exams and have enough CATS [Credit Accumulation Transfer System] points to go to a good Uni.

Q9 Consider these questions about NVC:

* When you are explaining a concept to your learners, what NVC signs do you look for (from your learners) to ascertain if they are listening and understanding what you are saying?

- When your learners are speaking to you, what NVC signs do you give them to show that you are interested in them, understand what they are saying and that you value their contribution?

Q10 Appropriate language:

a) If your learners are discussing some personal event, do you join in?
b) Do you use 'text speak' when writing?
c) Do you use language and written words that your learners won't understand?

Q11 Give yourself a score from one to five for each of the following points. Five is excellent, one is poor.

- Can you write formal letters correctly?
- Are you confident and competent when writing on the board and producing handouts?
- Can you spell most words correctly?
- Can you speak to your senior management team with confidence?
- Do you have an extensive range of vocabulary?

A SUMMARY OF KEY POINTS

In this chapter you have learned about:

> your current ability to communicate effectively;

> using a range of communication techniques with a range of people for different purposes;

> examples of non-verbal communication;

> reasons for considering appropriate meta-language;

> reasons why confidentiality is important.

REFERENCES AND FURTHER READING REFERENCES AND FURTHER READING

Gravells A (2007) *Preparing to Teach in the Lifelong Learning Sector*. Exeter: Learning Matters.
Gravells A (2009) *Principles and Practice of Assessment in the Lifelong Learning Sector.* Exeter: Learning Matters.
Gravells A & Simpson S (2008) *Planning and Enabling Learning in the Lifelong Learning Sector.* Exeter: Learning Matters.

Websites
Access For All (2001): **www.dcsf.gov.uk/curriculum_literacy/access/**
Adult Literacy Core Curriculum, (2008): **www.dfes.gov.uk/curriculum_literacy/ tree/writing/writingcomp/l2/**
Businessballs (2009): **www.businessballs.com**
Data Protection Act (1988): **www.opsi.gov.uk/Acts/Acts1998/ukpga_19980029_en_1**
Freedom of Information Acts (2000): **www.opsi.gov.uk/Acts/acts2000/ukpga_20000036_en_1**
Guidance to Teachers and Employers, LLUK (Sept. 2008): Evidencing Personal Skills in Literacy and Numeracy: **www.lluk.org/documents/evidencing-personal-skills-requirements.pdf**
Minimum Core (2007): **www.lluk.org.uk/minimum_core_may_2007_3rd.pdf**
Qualifications and Curriculum Authority (2004) Communication Key Skill, QCA: **www.qca.org.uk/14-19/11-16-schools/index_s5-3-using-key-skills.htm**

2
Reading

By the end of this chapter you should be able to:

- **use and reflect on a range of reading strategies to interpret texts and to locate information or meaning;**
- **identify methods to source information, including the internet;**
- **identify and record the key information or messages contained within reading material using note-taking techniques.**

This chapter and the objectives contribute to the Minimum Core requirements:
Part B; Personal Language Skills: Reading.

This chapter contributes towards the following LLUK standards:
AS4, AS5, AS7.1, AP7.2, CP3.4.
Also relevant to the Adult Core Curriculum Rtl/2.

Key information

For some people reading is a pleasure, something that they do in their spare time. Many people pack their suitcases with a variety of reading material when they go on holiday and they enjoy having the time to read. Other people, however, find reading to be a chore, something that they do only when they have to.

Whatever your opinion of reading, it is something that as a teacher you have to do probably every single day of your working life. You will need to read to be informed and you need to read to communicate. You will need to read subject-specific literature. You will also need to read learners' work, emails, letters and a plethora of other, generally informative, correspondence. There may be times when you need to read aloud to either your learners, colleagues or others within the field of education.

Furthermore, you will need to read and to understand what it is that you are reading. You need to be able to discern between fact and theory, particularly because you have a responsibility towards your learners to ensure that any information that you give them is correct. You need to be able to judge how appropriate the information is for its intended audience and you need, when necessary, to be able to read and summarise the reading into your own words.

Some people read very slowly and follow each word on the page, while other people can seemingly read a page of information extremely quickly and are able to get the gist of the information contained on the page. People who can do this tend to move their eyes down the centre of the page and use their peripheral vision to see words at the beginning and end of lines.

Reading well and with competence requires practice. Some people start reading at a very early age and are skilful readers throughout their adult life. Others begin to develop this skill only in their adult life when their job, or some other reason, requires them to do so.

Some people who do not consider themselves to be competent at reading often practise and develop their reading skills by reading aloud and by breaking down any polysyllabic words into single syllables. This might sound both tedious and possibly childlike but it is a process that, with practice, should enhance your ability to read.

It is also useful to have a good dictionary available. A good dictionary is useful for finding out how to pronounce words as well as providing the meaning and spelling of words.

If you have a diagnosed reading disability or if you think that you have an issue with reading that is more significant or serious than that attributed to lack of practice, it may be a good idea to ask for some support from your organisation. This support can come in many guises, including diagnosing any underlying cause or by providing necessary equipment or perhaps even a support assistant.

Reading strategies

Skilled readers develop strategies to enable them to locate information and to get the gist of the information very quickly. Teachers need to do this because their job role often means that they need to be able to access information quickly. Strategies that people use include:

- *skimming* – sweeping the surface of the page for information;
- *scanning* – picking out the information that is relevant to your requirements;
- *summarising* – putting the information found into logical order.

Skimming pages (electronic or hard copy) involves quickly looking down the page, passing your eyes along and down the page, to see if it looks interesting in relation to your topic. Using this technique enables you to obtain the gist of the reading and of the information. When skimming for information that may be of interest to you it may be useful to read the chapter, topic or sub-headings first and then skim the information between the headings that you consider may be of interest to you.

How often do you pick up a magazine, novel or other book of interest and look quickly through the pages to see if it is of interest? How often do you search for information using the internet and look down the pages to see if they contain the information that you are seeking?

When you do this you have used the skill of skimming. Make a special point of applying the same skill, if necessary, to any specific reading task.

Scanning follows skimming. If, when skimming the pages, you consider the information to be of interest you scan the pages for more specific detail, certain key words or main points of interest. Your eyes, mind and concentration focus on the words that you want to see and they ignore the words that you are not interested in.

For example, you will probably use the technique of scanning when looking for a specific name in a telephone directory. You look for the initial letter, or possibly for the first few letters, and ignore all of the other information on the page. However, when scanning for information out of a book that is more interesting than a list of names, it is easy to become distracted. You may stop scanning to read some information that you have found to be interesting but is not relevant to what you should be looking for. Have you ever searched for information on the internet only to find yourself consuming valuable time reading information that, although interesting, is not relevant to your requirements?

Summarising follows scanning. If, when you have scanned the pages, you still consider the information of sufficient interest you will read the pages, or appropriate sections of the pages, that are relevant to your topic. You then summarise this information using your own words.

Other strategies that are sometimes used when reading to obtain information:

- looking at the table of contents;
- looking at the index pages;
- looking at chapter headings and sub-headings;
- looking at pictures, diagrams and other visual representations within texts;
- reading word for word. You should do this when reading instructions, for example examination instructions, a recipe, or how to use electronic equipment.

Proofreading your work

Proofreading can be a very tedious task. However, failing to proofread work could have disastrous results or make others perceive your work as being sloppy because they often note errors within it.

Mistakes can happen even when you give a task your undivided attention. When you are doing several tasks at once or rushing a task, mistakes are almost inevitable.

Develop the habit of always re-reading your work. This includes re-reading emails. If you have written a time, a room number, a figure or some other important information incorrectly, the consequences of the error could be serious. Imagine that you deposit a million pounds that you have won into your bank only to find out later that the cashier had missed a few noughts from the end of the amount when they were typing it into your account. The bank's computer system shows that you have one thousand deposited instead of one million – possibly because the cashier did not re-read his work.

Other, less significant, errors that can be spotted and amended through proofreading are spelling errors. A computer's spell check facility cannot recognise words that are spelt correctly but are nevertheless a mistake. For example, typing 'deport' when you should have typed 'report'.

Re-read and proofread so that your work is 100 per cent accurate.

Readability of material

You can check that the material and information that you give your learners to read is at the correct level for their current reading age. The length, complexity and use of polysyllabic words determine the suitability of information for different reading ages. The following processes enable an accurate assessment for this purpose.

Simple Measure of Gobbledygook index (SMOG)

A SMOG index enables you to calculate the readability of your reading material, handouts that you produce or any other written work. It can be calculated by:

- taking a sample of ten sentences;
- counting the number of words with three or more syllables;
- multiplying your answer by ten;
- finding the square root of this number;
- adding eight.

Frequency of Gobbledygook index (FOG)

A FOG index is calculated by:

- selecting a passage of 100 words;
- counting the number of complete sentences;
- counting the words in each of the complete sentences;
- finding the average sentence length by dividing the number of words in all of the complete sentences by the number of complete sentences;
- counting the number of words of three or more syllables;
- adding the length and number, then multiply by 0.4 and add 5.

The above manual systems are useful for hard copy material. However, as most of your work will probably be word-processed you should be able to check the readability of your material electronically by using the appropriate functions on your word-processing programme; this is usually via the tools, spelling, grammar and readability functionality buttons. More information relating to readability of information can be found using the internet, and some websites are listed at the end of this chapter.

Identify methods to source information

As a teacher you will need to find information from a variety of sources including from reading material such as:

- journals
- books
- internet/intranet
- CD-ROMS
- magazines
- newspapers

Technology is fast paced and constantly changing and so is information. You need to decide what it is you need to find out, how current the information needs to be and what are the most appropriate sources that are available to you.

The internet, otherwise known as the World Wide Web (www), has a vast amount of information that is quickly accessible. However, the information is not necessarily well researched and may not be based on grounded research or factual information. You need to consider how credible the person or organisation who has posted the information is within the field of the topic that they have written about. You could do this by looking at other work that has been posted by the same person or by looking on the website of the organisation. Furthermore, it is often a good idea to choose sites that are recognisable, for example academic sites (ending in .ac), government sites (ending in .gov). If you want information that is relevant to the UK, you can select this option on the search engine that you use.

Furthermore, you may consider combining keywords when searching for information. Using single keywords may generate too many records, although using many words, perhaps more than four, may narrow the search to the extent that very few records are found.

You may also want to include a timeframe for the information you are trying to find, or you may want to find a specific type of file (Powerpoint, text, etc.). Most search engines should have the facility to allow you to do this. An advanced search strategy provides you with an opportunity to define your search in more detail.

When you read information from books, magazines, journals, newspapers or other hard-copy material, you might need to consider the currency of the information and if what you are reading is still applicable or if it has been superseded by other information. For example, consider the edition of any book that you are reading. If you are reading information in relation to a topic that changes due to technological, geographical or political changes an old edition, out-of-date magazine or newspaper may provide inaccurate information.

Wherever you get your information from you do need to check for any bias or if the information has been written from a particular point of view. For example, differing ideologies by people of different political persuasions can provide quite different slants on exactly the same facts. As a teacher you have the responsibility to ensure that your learners are provided with accurate information, and if the information is from a particular viewpoint you need to acknowledge this. You should always be mindful of the accuracy and appropriateness of any reading material that you are reading and may use in the classroom or within your teaching environment.

When searching for information from a specific known source you may find it useful to search by:

- author
- title
- publisher
- ISBN number
- subject

Remember that searching for information can be time-consuming. Having a range of strategies can be very useful in speeding up the process and indeed making it possible to find information from the internet.

HINTS AND TIPS
When searching on the internet you can:

- link keywords using 'and/or' to narrow or widen the search;
- use an asterisk (*) to replace missing letters/to truncate words;
- select a time period for your information (e.g. 2007–2008);
- repeat your search using different key words if necessary.

Identifying key information

When reading to obtain information you often need to record the information that you have found. This is to enable you to use the information towards further searches or to summarise the information for use with your learners, or within your wider teaching role. There are several strategies that can be used to do this:

- *Identifying key words* – It is useful to note the most significant and important key words within the information that you are reading in case you need to do any further searches.

- *Summarising/paraphrasing* – If the information is relevant it can be useful to summarise and paraphrase it. This has a dual purpose. It provides a record of the information that you have read and it also aids your comprehension by having to consider it in your own words.

- *Annotating and note-taking* – You can annotate information by using a highlighter pen over key words and phrases and also by writing your own comments beside the information that you are reading. If you need to refer to specific points within the information at a later date, the highlighted areas will stand out (and the annotated notes will help you to recall your thoughts on it).

HINTS AND TIPS

When you take notes ensure that they are legible. Often notes that you think you will understand when making them make no sense when you come to decipher them at a later date.

Keep your notes where you know that you will be able to find them.

Note-taking is a useful strategy to record key information. Note-taking can also help to improve your memory by giving you more opportunity to receive the information (i.e. when you make the notes and then again when you read the notes).

Note-taking can be done in prose or a checklist format. It can also be carried out using a mind/diagrammatic map technique. An important point is to ensure that you record accurately where you have taken the information from. You may need to access it at a later date or you may need to present the information (or extracts from it) in written or verbal format. If you do this you must say where the information is from because if you do not you are plagiarising. Plagiarism is when you use an author's written work or ideas without acknowledging him or her, particularly if you try and pass off this work as your own. This is so serious that authors can accuse the user of their work of theft. Universities can also fail your assignment if you do not cite your sources.

HINTS AND TIPS

- Reading backwards can help you to proofread your work. This is because it disrupts your familiarity with the information, thereby providing you with an opportunity to spot any errors more easily.
- If possible leave your work alone for a few days and then re-read it. Very often giving yourself this space provides an opportunity for you to re-read your work with a fresh pair of eyes.

Key questions

Now have a go at the exercises.

These exercises are designed to help you test yourself in this topic. Some are reflective questions and thus require you to discuss your potential answers with colleagues/tutors. Some require you to use a dictionary, spell checker or other resources that will be available to you. Work through the exercises and note your answers on a separate sheet. The answers can be found at the back of the book.

Read the following passage and then complete all of the exercises below.

The pace of change since incorporation has been rapid; in 2001 the first Further Education (FE) lecturers' qualification regulations were instigated, namely the FENTO (Further Education National Training Organisation) standards. These standards were an attempt to standardise the quality of the workforce and equip lecturers with skills, knowledge and attributes that could be measured. Up until this point any requirements for teaching qualifications had been set by individual institutions (IfL, 2006, page 2). Further research and political discourse brought about other reports including OFSTED (2003), all of which noted that clearer standards were required. In 2004 a further report 'Equipping our lecturers for the future', supported these previous findings. The aim of this report was to instigate further reform of FE lecturer training and to note the replacement of the FENTO standards with Lifelong Learning (LLUK) standards, which would ultimately enable lecturers to gain qualified lecturer, learning and skills (QTLS) status. The aim of this professional status is to rid the sector of its often referred to 'Cinderella Service' status' (Orr, 2008) and partially, to gain parity with schools in relation to professional status and financial remuneration (page 97). In 2005, the Foster Review (Realising the Potential) provided a critical appraisal of workforce development within FE and in response to this the Government presented a White Paper 'Raising skills improving life chances' (2006). This pivotal paper included the introduction of a mandatory registration system (not dissimilar to schools' registration to the GTC (General Teaching Council) and the requirement to undertake 30 hours annual continual professional development (CPD). CPD is a requirement of several professionalised bodies, for example solicitors and doctors. In September, 2007 the Institute for Learning (IfL) issued regulations within ITT (Initial Teacher Training) to ensure the conferral of professional status and the need, by March 2008, for all lecturers to have registered with them (IfL, 2006). The introduction of these regulations was seen, by IfL (2007), to provide 'a vision for professional development that is meaningful and responsive to the needs of an incredibly diverse workforce' (Inform, 2007, page 2).

21 Using the information in the passage above, consider what the following abbreviations mean.

1. FENTO
2. FE
3. CPD
4. IfL
5. QTLS
6. LLUK

22 Using the information in the passage above, identify which one of the statements overleaf is correct?

a. The current standards are provided by FENTO.
b. The current standards are provided by OFSTED.
c. The current standards are provided by LLUK.
d. The current standards are provided by IfL.

Q3 Using the information from the passage above, find the dates pertaining to the information provided in the questions below.

1. An aim of the standards was to gain parity with schools.
2. OFSTED indicated that clearer standards were necessary.
3. All lecturers needed to be registered with the IfL.
4. The first regulations were put into place.
5. A report supported OFSTED's findings.
6. A critical appraisal of the workforce was provided.

Q4 Consider the following statements and note which one applies most appropriately to the information in the passage above.

a) Awarding Bodies, regulations and reports all note the importance of regulating a professionalised school system.
b) School teachers are required to register with the IfL and undertake 30 hours of CPD annually.
c) To have parity with schools, regulations and reports were written to enable the FE workforce to become professionalised and regulated.
d) To meet the needs of a diverse workforce, regulations and reports were written to enable the FE workforce to become professionalised and regulated.

Q5 Using the information from the passage above, for whom would the information be most appropriate from the examples given below?

a. Principals
b. Heads of departments
c. Trainee teachers
d. Teachers

Q6 If you were searching for information in relation to the assignment title 'Teaching in the Lifelong Learning Sector: an interesting experience and professional career', what key words would you use within your search?

Q7 Choose one answer for each of the following questions:

1) What is plagiarism?
    a. A quick reading strategy.
    b. Not attributing information to the appropriate author.
    c. Not attributing information to the appropriate timeframe.
    d. A readability strategy.

2) What is a FOG Index?
    a. Formula of gobbledygook.
    b. Fact or gist.
    c. Frequency of gobbledygook.
    d. A type of weather.

3) What is skimming?
   a. Editing text.
   b. Looking for key words from within text.
   c. Scrolling your eyes down the page in search of key words.
   d. Searching for the gist from a piece of text.

4) What is scanning?
   a. Copying a piece of text.
   b. Scrolling your eyes down the page to get the gist of the information.
   c. Looking for key words from within text.
   d. Searching for the gist from a piece of text.

Q8 Read the following words and provide a meaning for them. Use a dictionary to check your answers:

- dichotomy
- esoteric
- eclectic
- nuance
- phenomena
- hyperbole
- notion
- regulatory

Q9 Use a thesaurus (electronic or hard copy) and look up a different word that means the same as those listed below:

- infiltrate
- opposite
- exaggerate
- idea
- varied
- experience
- policy
- similarly

Q10 Search for information relating to gaining QTLS and then answer the following questions:

1. Which professional body is overseeing the process of QTLS?
2. How long does someone working within the Lifelong Learning Sector take to gain QTLS?
3. What do you need to achieve prior to acquiring QTLS status?
4. What do you need to retain OTLS status?

A SUMMARY OF KEY POINTS

In this chapter you have learned about:

> a range of reading strategies to interpret texts and to locate information or meaning;

> how to identify methods to source information, including the internet;

> methods that can be used to record the key information or messages contained within reading material using note-taking techniques.

REFERENCES AND FURTHER READING REFERENCES AND FURTHER READING

Gravells A (2007) Preparing *to Teach in the Lifelong Learning Sector*. Exeter: Learning Matters.

Gravells A (2009) *Principles and Practice of Assessment in the Lifelong Learning Sector.* Exeter: Learning Matters.

Gravells A & Simpson S (2008) *Planning and Enabling Learning in the Lifelong Learning Sector*. Exeter: Learning Matters.

Institute for Learning (2006) 'Towards a New Professionalism', Annual Conference Papers. London.

Orr K (2008) Room for improvement? The impact of compulsory professional development for teaching in England's further education sector, *Journal of Further Education*, 34 (1).

Reece S & Walker R (2008), *Teacher Training and Learning, A Practical Guide, 6th Edn*. Sunderland: British Education Publishers.

Websites

Access For All (2001): **www.dcsf.gov.uk/curriculum_literacy/access/**

Adult Literacy Core Curriculum (2008): **www.dfes.gov.uk/curriculum_literacy/ tree/writing/writingcomp/l2/**

DIUS, Readwrite (2008): **www.dfes.gov.uk/readwriteplus**

Guidance to Teachers and Employers, LLUK (Sept. 2008), Evidencing Personal Skills, in Literacy and Numeracy: **www.lluk.org/ documents/evidencing-personal-skills-requirements.pdf**

Minimum Core (2007): **www.lluk.org.uk/minimum_core_may_2007_3rd.pdf**

Skillswise (2008): **www.bbc.co/skillswise www.lluk.org/documents/evidencing-personal-skills-requirements.pdf**

For testing readability: **www.online-utility.org/english/readability_test_and_improve.jsp** and **www.lct.ac.uk/supportforlearning/hidden_disability/pracguide2_readability.pdf**

DFES (2005) Equipping Our Teachers for the Future: **www.dcsf.gov.uk/furthereducation/uploads/documents/equippingourteachersforthefuture-115-161.pdf**

DIUS (2006) Raising Skills, Improving Life Chances: **www.publications.dcsf.gov.uk/ default.aspx?PageFunction=productiondetails&PageMode= publications&ProductId=Cm%25206476**

Foster A (Nov. 2005) Realising the Potential: **www.dcsf.gov.uk/furthereducation/ uploads/documents/REALISING06.pdf**

OFSTED (2003) The Initial Training of Further Education Teachers 2003: **www.ofsted.gov.uk/ Ofsted-home/Publications-and-research/Browse-all-by/Education/Teachers-and-teacher- training?query=teacher+training+further+ education2003&SearchSectionID=12**

Inform (2007) *JISC*, Issue 19: **www.jisc.ac.uk/publications/publications/publications/ inform19.aspx**

3
Writing conventions

Key information

As a teacher you will be required to write a variety of correspondence. It is important that you are able to do this correctly and competently so that people can read your work and also understand the content of your work.

What are writing conventions?

Writing conventions are styles of writing that you should, or could, use when corresponding with others. The appropriate convention is dependent upon the type of correspondence that you are sending and to whom it is being sent.

This correspondence could include writing letters, reports, emails and filling in forms.

Using correct writing conventions

As a teacher you are often judged on your ability to be professional. Being professional includes the way you present your work and any correspondence that you send. For example, the way you present your curriculum vitae (CV) will be noticed by any recipient. Many CVs are discarded immediately because they are not presented professionally or they contain spelling or grammatical errors.

Plan and draft your writing
You should plan all correspondence carefully. The recipient forms an impression of you by the style, layout and language that you use within informal and formal correspondence.

You should consider carefully the main points that you want to say, the tone that you want to convey and the message or information that you want to give. Furthermore, consider how the recipient will perceive you by your style of writing.

Planning and drafting includes:

- organising your information by putting it into note/map/diagram format;
- considering what information needs to go first, second, etc.;
- considering the structure and type of language that you need to use.

Some people prefer to handwrite their work prior to typing it up on the computer. Other people use the computer to type their draft. Use whichever method you prefer but always check your work for coherence, grammar, spelling, correct punctuation and presentation.

It is possible that after the letter or email had been sent you noticed that you had missed out some important point that you wanted to make or perhaps you noticed a spelling error. If you have written an assignment without drafting or planning it first you have possibly found that it is disjointed, repetitive, over or under the recommended words, or that you have not adhered to the criteria provided.

Judging the level of detail to include

Have you ever thought it annoying when someone speaks to you and they simply just *don't shut up*? They go on and on saying the same thing in a slightly different way on numerous occasions or they provide you with so much unnecessary detail that you do not know what the point is that they are really trying to make. When using a written format to communicate with someone it is possible to give so much information that you either run out of words for the main points or the main points are lost within the mass of information. Some people also make the mistake of repeating the same information but in differing ways. Moreover, busy people can get irritated by having to read many words with apparently no meaning, so if you want to impress someone remember to be succinct with words.

As a teacher, when you are asked to write something, for example a letter or report, it is important that you are very precise about what you are saying. Providing ambiguous or excessive information will not give the reader a good impression of you. Providing inaccurate information could be disastrous.

When writing assignments it is important that you remain focused on the key points. Assignments are often given a word limit – the reason for this is that the Awarding Body is looking for quality, not quantity, of words.

To write concisely consider if you could replace a group of words with one, or possibly two, words. For example, avoid lengthy statements such as 'due to the fact that'; instead use 'because'.

If you were placing an advertisement in your local paper and there was a cost for each word you would need to be very concise while still ensuring that the reader knew exactly what you were advertising. The same principle applies to many other forms of written communication. Check any work for repetition.

Presenting information

You need to put information into a logical sequence. For example, if you are describing or explaining something, you may need to provide some background information to ensure that the reader understands the content and purpose of your correspondence. For example, if you need to write a report about an incidence of bullying that you had witnessed outside your classroom, you may need to say what alerted you to this prior to you actually going out of the classroom to address the incident (e.g. you may have heard shouting).

If you were writing to persuade someone to do or give you something, you would need to express your ideas and comments in a sequence that is most likely to convince the reader of your request. For instance, if you wanted to persuade the Resource Manager to provide you with a laptop computer, you would initially state the main reasons why you needed one. You might follow this with one or two less important reasons and finally end with another strong reason for the need of a laptop. You might support your request with some facts or research. You also need to anticipate the counter argument that the recipient might make and ensure that you cover these points in favour of your request. The use of persuasive language is a method that many retail outlets use when sending out sales brochures.

HINTS AND TIPS

Use the first paragraph to very briefly explain the reason for the correspondence.

Use the middle paragraph(s) to provide the details. Ensure that facts are accurate and that no essential information is omitted.

Use the final paragraph to summarise the message and to end the correspondence in a courteous way.

Different styles for different purposes

As well as considering the sequence within any correspondence, it is necessary to consider your style of writing. Syntax, register and vocabulary are important considerations when writing. All of these depend upon the purpose, audience and context of your correspondence. Some correspondence follows standard structures, for example letters, agendas, reports and minutes of meetings.

Syntax is the way that you order your words and construct your sentences. As with your vocabulary it is important that you consider the person, or people, to whom you are writing. Complex sentences are suitable when writing to a principal, line manager, many parents or writing assignments. However, they may not be suitable for some learners and for some parents. A complex sentence contains a verb, an independent clause and at least one dependent clause or, put more simply, two sentences put together (e.g. 'The learner received a good grade, and was extremely happy about this').

Register is the term used to explain different ways of speaking and writing to people. For example, you might write a very different note or letter to a good friend or colleague about being absent from work than you would if you were writing about the same thing to your Head of Department.

Vocabulary needs to be considered in relation to the person or persons to whom you are writing. For example, the vocabulary that you use when preparing handouts for learners aged 14–19 will possibly need to be different to the vocabulary that you use when writing formal letters.

'Hi Sue 4got 2 go 2 mtg yestday. Did u bring yr notes bac. If so cn u bring thm 2 my office l8tr!'

The above message is one of many examples that could be used to illustrate the use of written text when using a mobile phone. This style has become acceptable by many people in the world today because of the necessity to use limited characters because of cost and space. The 'audience' in this example would probably be a close colleague. The purpose would be an informal and friendly request for some information. While you may text a close colleague, as a general rule you should never use 'text' in any form of professional correspondence. It is very poor practice and not everyone can read text language.

Coherence

When using any written format to communicate you need to join key points together within paragraphs. Importantly, however, the key points need to connect or follow a structure to enable each paragraph to flow onto the paragraph following it. You may find it easier to write your ideas down first and then consider how you want to link the ideas and in what order you want to put them.

A further consideration is the words and phrases that you use to express your ideas. If possible write down what it is you want or need to say and then consider any improvements or amendments that you want to make to your words and phrases afterwards.

The words and phrases that you use need to convey your thoughts, information or ideas to the reader. Make sure that you use words, expressions and phrases that 'suit the reader' so that the meaning is clear. If you are not sufficiently precise and coherent the reader may interpret your message incorrectly.

Emails are notorious for mis-communicating messages. The sender often writes them quickly without considering ambiguities, over-familiarisation and misunderstandings that the reader may find in the message.

Different text types

Emails

Emails have replaced the use of memorandums and also often replace formal letters. They can also, of course, be used as an electronic courier to send formal letters, reports, forms and other written forms of correspondence.

When writing emails you should:

- use a subject heading to allow the reader an opportunity to know if they want to open the email or not;
- always check your spelling before sending an email. People will notice your errors even if they do not notice their own when they send emails;
- check that the email will make sense to the reader. Emails are notorious for mis-communicating messages, often because of the speed and lack of thought that goes into sending them;
- consider the salutation (greeting) that you begin the email with. Unless you know the recipient of the email personally and as a friend, avoid 'hi', either use 'Hello' or simply

state the recipient's name. This may seem a little formal but it is better than the recipient of the email thinking that you are a little over-familiar.

Language used within emails is generally less formal than if it were a letter being posted or a memorandum being delivered. However, it is important that you consider to whom the email is being sent. The tone and the formality of the email may differ depending upon who the receiver is.

End emails in a courteous way, for example;

- Regards
- Best wishes

Emails rarely begin and end in a typical letter convention style (i.e. they do not begin with 'Dear Sir/Madam' and end with 'Yours faithfully').

Emails often get circulated to other people. Do not end formal or semi-formal emails (to colleagues and line managers for example) with 'love' even if they are a good friend.

Letter writing
The internet may have reduced the amount of letters that we now write but there are still plenty of times when a letter, posted or attached to an email, is the only appropriate form of communication. Although in a professional capacity you may not need to write many letters, when you do it is important that they follow the correct convention and that the grammar, punctuation and spelling are correct. Of course, before the wide-spread use of computers a teacher would often only draft a letter and a secretary would type the letter for her.

There are several types of letters that you might write during your professional career, for example:

- applying for publication;
- providing a reference;
- seeking employment;
- to another academic institution;
- writing to a newspaper.

You should always use the correct writing convention for letters.

Letter layout
If you are writing a letter in relation to your work, use the organisation's headed paper (containing their name, address and telephone details) and follow the convention detailed below:

- If the letter is confidential then mark it as such (i.e. Confidential).
- The name of the recipient, e.g. Mr F. Bloggs, Mrs G. Bloggs, Ms C. Bloggs, David Bloggs.
- The address and postcode of the recipient.
- The date; this is usually written in full, e.g. 10 December 2009.
- The salutation, e.g. Dear Sir, Dear Madam, Dear Mr, Dear Mrs, Dear Susan, Dear David.
- Subject heading, e.g. *Reference for Joe Bloggs* (*note the underscore*).
- The main body of the letter — what it is you want to say. Leave one clear line space between paragraphs. Use a straight left margin, set at approximately 2.5cm (1").

Generally, most organisations use an unjustified (ragged) right-hand margin, set at 2.5cm (1").

- The complimentary close, e.g. Yours faithfully, Yours sincerely.
- Your name; note that between the complimentary close and your name, leave five clear line spaces for your signature to be handwritten within the space provided.
- The name of the organisation, e.g. Suburbia College of Further Education.
- If there are any attachments/enclosures with the letter, type 'Enc.' or 'Encs' at the foot.
- Cc, e.g. the name(s) of the person or people who received a copy of the letter; note: that although a carbon copy is no longer used because we can now do multiple print-outs or photocopies, the term 'cc' has been retained.

Most people now type correspondence using a semi-blocked style. This is when every line of typing starts at the left hand margin with a clear line space being left between paragraphs. Some people have a fully blocked right hand margin as well, but this can lead to too many spaces between words so is not recommended.

Does it really matter?

It is possibly true that some people may not notice, or even know, if a letter is written correctly. However, some people will notice, and will know, if the letter is incorrect. The recipient of the letter will form an opinion of you, or at least your ability to write correctly. So yes, it really does matter that you can write a letter correctly.

Even if you know the person whom you are writing to, for example a parent, learner or moderator, you need to avoid being too friendly or familiar. The fact that you feel it necessary to write a letter rather than to send an email or to use the telephone to communicate with them indicates the necessity of a formal, or at least semi-formal, approach.

It is important to keep a professional tone when writing any formal correspondence. Avoid adding any personal comments that fall outside of the reason for writing the letter – it may be that the letter is shown to other people.

Avoid the use of colloquial language (i.e. language that we use in everyday communication with our friends and colleagues). For example:

- he's really doing my head in;
- it would be cool if you could attend;
- you know;
- to be honest.

Can you think of any more colloquialisms?

HINTS AND TIPS

If ever you need to sign a letter on behalf of anyone else, you should place the letters 'pp' before your signature. These letters are Latin for *per procurationem*, which means 'for and on behalf of'.

Report writing

As a teacher you will be asked to write many types of reports. For example, end of term/year learner reports, self-assessment reports (SARs), self-evaluation document (SEDs) and incident reports. Reports are about providing facts clearly and concisely.

Sometimes within a report, possibly in the summary, you may also need to provide your opinion based upon the facts provided. If you are required to do this, you need to ensure that the reader of the report knows that it is your opinion that you are stating. The reader may be making important decisions in relation to your report.

There are two main types of reports: the formal report and the informal report.

An informal report may be used at team meetings or as a brief to your line manager. However, remember that people may ask for an informal report but they will still expect a professional report.

An informal report is often a bullet point list of information and facts. It might have a summary or conclusion.

The formal report may be a submission to the Principal, line manager, or external agency. It may be used in meetings. It may be filed for future use by others.

A report usually consists of:

- the title of the report;
- terms of reference – this is usually a short statement of the reason for the report and the name(s) of the person(s) requesting it;
- process – this states the sources of the information;
- several main headings – giving the details of the report;
- sub-headings if appropriate – giving more details of the report;
- summary or conclusion – a short statement summarising the main points within the report and, if requested, providing an opinion;
- recommendations – what action, if any, you consider needs taking;
- the date of the report;
- your signature;
- a circulation list – listing the recipients of the report.

When you write a report the headings above are a useful guide. Consider the information that you need to put in a report and think about a logical sequence for it. Sometimes you are already provided with headings to use within a report – if so, use them.

Consider any issues of confidentiality. Under the Data Protection and Freedom of Information Acts access is permitted to information by any interested party – that is anyone whose name appears within the report or anyone who may be considered under the Acts to have a right to the information.

If you have referred to any literature or to any discussion or interview, ensure that you acknowledge the source(s). Literature should be cited and referenced using the Harvard system of referencing. If you are unsure how to do this, there are many suitable sites on the internet that will provide information relating to this.

Other forms of writing

Notices
You may be asked to write or design a notice for a special event, for example an open evening. If so consider the following:

- where is the notice to be placed? This information is necessary so that you can consider the size and layout of the notice;

- write the notice using words that everyone will be able to understand (i.e. avoid jargon);
- use a large, sans serif font (Arial 12 or 14 is popular);
- use a picture if appropriate;
- leave plenty of white space to aid readability;
- proofread the notice. You will be most embarrassed, and could be perceived to be unprofessional, if your notice is displayed and there are spelling or grammatical errors;
- make it your responsibility to ensure that the notice has been removed when the information is no longer required.

A useful acronym that is sometimes used by people with a background in business is AIDA, which means:

- Attention
- Interest
- Desire
- Action

When preparing a notice, consider capturing the *attention* and *interest* of the intended audience. Once you have this, the notice should bring about a *desire* for your intended audience to *act*, for example, to buy the tickets or attend the event that the notice is advertising.

Forms

Within your teaching career you will be asked to complete many forms. It is possible that some forms will be returned to you because they are not completed correctly. Completing them correctly the first time is an effective use of time.

Many forms can now be completed online. The same format is used for online and hand-written reports.

- Read the instructions for completing the form.
- Forms are often completed using capital letters.
- Ensure that all of the form is completed correctly with no information missed out.
- Sign the form if the form states that this is necessary.
- If you are handwriting the form, look at the information required before writing anything and consider carefully what you need to write.
- It is not advisable to cross out, use white-out liquid or an eraser when completing a form.
- Handwritten forms are generally completed using a pen, with black ink, to aid readability and to help when photocopying the report.

A few other comments

Take note of the comments that have been made throughout this chapter about writing conventions. However, there are several other things to consider when communicating with someone using a written format.

Never start a letter, email or similar with 'I am writing' – it is quite obvious that you are writing. Alternatives could be:

- With reference to our telephone call today …

- I am enquiring …
- I wish to inform you …

Never end a formal or semi-formal letter, email or similar with:

- Love

Never use any words that you do not know the meaning of. Rather than making you look intelligent, using words inappropriately could make you look foolish.

Avoid using jargon or technical words that the reader of your correspondence may not understand. If you do need to use a technical word, ensure that you explain its meaning the first time that you use it. (Note: there is a glossary of terms at the back of this book explaining words and acronyms that may be unfamiliar to the reader.)

Keep any instructions, descriptions or directions as simple as possible and include diagrams if necessary.

Do not 'mix business with pleasure' when you are writing. Remember your correspondence may be shown to other people.

Avoid common errors and confusion

Knowing a few basic rules can prevent unnecessary errors being made. Sometimes these errors are caused as a result of how we speak. We may not have learned to connect certain words together or we may use the wrong connectors.

A fairly common mistake is the use of 'have' and 'of', for example:

- *could of* – when it should be *could have*
- *should of* – when it should be *should have*
- *would of* – when it should be *would have*
- *must of* – when it should be *must have*

One reason that this mistake is made is because when speaking words are contracted, (e.g. could've, should've). The sound of these contracted words is sometimes misheard (as *could of, should of*).

Another two words that are sometimes confused are 'can' and 'will'.

In formal English the word 'can' refers to the ability to do something, for example:

I can teach the English learners how to use apostrophes.

However, it is often used in the form of a question when you want someone to do something, for example:

Can you cover my class tonight?

The person you are asking may well be able to cover the class (they have the ability to do so), but this does not mean that they will cover the class. The question should really be:

Will you cover my class tonight?

> **HINTS AND TIPS**
> *Neither, either, nor* and *or* sometimes get confused.
>
> - 'neither' is used with 'nor' but not with 'or' (e.g. *Neither* Jason *nor* his brother went to college).
> - 'either' is used with 'or' but not with 'nor' (e.g. 'You can *either* take the DTLLS route *or* ask for information about the CTLLS route.'

In formal English the word 'may' refers to permission or a probability, for example:

> *'May I leave the class early so that I can go to the dentist, please?'*
>
> *'Leslie may go to the University this afternoon, providing that he finishes his class on time.'*

When is it 'that' and when is it 'which'?

'That' and 'which' are two frequently used words and often they are interchangeable with the exception of when you are referring to people.

When referring to people you should never use the pronoun 'which'. For example:

- The teachers *which* went to the meeting said that there was a good attendance. ('Which' is wrong in this context.)
- The teachers *that* went to the meeting said that there was a good attendance. ('That' is used correctly in this sentence.)

Another use of 'that' and 'which' is that the former defines and the latter describes, for example:

> *The scheme of work that was excellent was given to the Ofsted Inspector. (There is more than one scheme of work but only the one that was excellent was given to the Ofsted Inspector.)*
>
> *The scheme of work, which was excellent, was given to the Ofsted Inspector. (There is only one scheme of work. It was excellent and was given to the Ofsted Inspector.)*

Appropriate fonts

The size and style of font that you use really does matter. It matters to your learners and it matters to you.

Your learners may have poor eyesight or reading difficulties. They may read your hand-outs using inadequate lighting facilities. Many organisations, including colleges, often recommend the use of a size 10 or 12 sans serif font (this means a font that has straight lines rather than curvy tails). This can aid clarity of reading.

Sans serif fonts are appropriate for formal correspondence because they are professional looking. A report to OFSTED, for example, will look more official using a straight font than it would if you used a font like Comic Sans. Likewise, assignments should be in a straight font. It has been noted in external examiners' reports that some ITT trainers do not use fonts that are suitable for academic writing.

Exceptions to using a sans serif font could be if you needed to use a specific font to illustrate meaning or an event. You would, in these instances, decide what was the most appropriate font size and style to use.

Correct grammar

As a teacher you will probably need to write official and formal correspondence. These letters will need to be constructed according to writing conventions and must be accurate and have cohesion.

Cohesion involves making links between sentences and ensuring that you use the correct tense and subject–verb agreement. If the subject is singular then the verb is singular; if the subject is plural then the verb is plural. This can be problematic specifically with the words 'has' and 'have' – these two words are often used incorrectly. For example:

> **EXAMPLE**
>
> - Some FE teachers work in the community and has made a real difference to the community.
> - Some FE teachers work in the community and have made a real difference to the community.
>
> The word 'some' is plural and therefore requires the word 'have'.

Use of pronouns

A pronoun replaces a noun. Examples of pronouns include:

Personal	Possessive	Relative	Reflexive
I	my	who	myself
me	his	whose	yourself
he	hers	that	himself
she	its	which	herself
it	yours	whoever	ourselves
him	ours	whichever	themselves
her	theirs		
you			
we			
they			
them			

It is a good idea to use pronouns to replace nouns in order to avoid too much repetition. However, you need to ensure that you are using them appropriately as they must not be attributed to the wrong person or people. For example:

> **EXAMPLE**
>
> *Ashraf liked the praise from Leslie and decided that, upon reflection, he was a good teacher.*
>
> In the example above it could be Ashraf or Leslie that was a good teacher. The pronoun 'he' should not have been used on this occasion and the sentence should have been written differently, for example:
>
> *Ashraf liked the praise from Leslie and decided that, upon reflection, Leslie was a good teacher.*

Using the pronouns 'I' and 'me'

Be careful to use 'I' and 'me' correctly when they take the form of objects and subjects:

EXAMPLE

Sally gave her homework to Bob and I.

This is incorrect because 'Bob and I' form a combined object. It should be:

Sally gave her homework to Bob and me.

A further example is:

Den and me went to the head teacher's lecture.

This is incorrect because 'Den and me' are the subjects. It should be:

Den and I went to the head teacher's lecture.

HINTS AND TIPS

If you are unsure about the use of 'I' and 'me' try the sentence with the other person missed out, for example:

- *Sally gave her homework to me* – you would not write or say 'Sally gave her homework to I.'
- *I went to the head teacher's lecture* – you would not write or say 'Me went to the head teacher's lecture.'

Always read your work and redo any part of it that is incorrect. If you are unsure of anything ask someone, refer to this book, or use a dictionary.

Key questions

Now have a go at the exercises.

These exercises are designed to help you test yourself in this topic. Some are reflective questions and thus require you to discuss your potential answers with colleagues/tutors. Some require you to use a dictionary, spell checker or other resources that will be available to you. Work through the exercises and note your answers on a separate sheet. The answers can be found at the back of the book.

Q1 Read the following draft extract and correct it:

Hi Dave,

D'ya think that it would be ok if I swopped classes with Liz next Wedesnday at 3pm. I will do her class the following Monday. I need too go to a proffesional development meeting on that day. Anyway let me know asap. The meeting is about behaviour management and might be of use to me when I am teaching.

Sue

Q2 Look at the paragraph below, which is 95 words long, and see if you can condense it to below 60 words, while retaining the information.

On Tuesday of last week (6 May 2008) I witnessed a group of learners fighting outside of my classroom, I was teaching Key Skills in RB3. I spoke to the learners and asked them what they were fighting about. Two of them, there were six learners altogether, said that they were sure two of the the others had stolen some money from them. I told them to go and see their course tutor to sort this out and I also told them that I would be reporting the incident to the Head of Department.

Q3 Write an email or letter to your line manager asking if you can go to a conference. The conference is for two days and is more expensive than the normal budget allowance for attending conferences. Consider any possible arguments against you going and ensure that you dispel any concerns in relation to these. Use persuasive language to stress the benefits of you going.

Check your answer with a friend, colleague or tutor.

Q4 Write an email to your line manager asking them for permission to close a class early due to it clashing with a professional development meeting that you have. The class is for two hours and you want to finish 15 minutes early. You can decide the subject, time of class and other appropriate information.

Check your answer with a friend, colleague or tutor.

Q5 Draft a reference for one of your learners who has been offered a full-time job as a trainee manager in a restaurant. Assume that the learner is suitable for the job and comment about some of their attributes within the body of the letter. The letter is confidential and should be addressed to Mr L. Tyler, The Garden Restaurant, 20 Church Road, Little Lawton, Sprigshire, SP5 2JM. It is also the custom of your college to send a copy of all references to the Learner Service Department.

Q6 You are the programme leader for GCSE English. Your line manager has asked you to provide a report relating to the first term (September–December) of a new programme. They will expect an account of learner numbers, the effectiveness of the induction process, current retention and any learner or programme issues. There may be other items that you think you need to include within the report to provide an accurate account of the first term of the programme. You are to present this report at a forthcoming meeting where it is expected that there will be at least eight other programme leaders – all of whom will also be presenting reports at the meeting in relation to their programmes.

Check your answer with a friend, colleague or tutor.

Q7 Design a notice for an open day due to take place in two weeks' time. You want to emphasise your department's courses and you want the notice to be attractive to learners, aged 14–19, and their parents.

Check your answer with a friend, colleague or tutor.

Q8 Answer 'yes' or 'no' to the statements below.

1. Letters that start with either Dear Sir or Dear Madam end in Yours sincerely.
2. You can use a more informal style when writing emails than you could with a letter.
3. Writing using text language is acceptable for all correspondence.
4. Letters that start with either Dear Mr … or Dear Mrs … end in Yours sincerely.
5. You should always write business letters using a formal writing convention.
6. It is acceptable to use colloquial language in formal writing.
7. A term of reference contains information as to why a report is being written.
8. You should always proofread your work.
9. A serif font is generally the preferred style for formal correspondence.
10. You should always use a large size font of at least 14 to aid readability.

Q9 Complete the sentences below using the words beneath.

Register is the ….. that you would use to convey meaning; whereas syntax is the way you …………. your sentences. Letters should always have a ……….. and a ……………. ……….. . Moreover a …….. and an …….. should always be included. A further point is that you should not use ……………in formal correspondence. Finally it is important that you ………..……… your work before sending it to the recipient.

- proofread
- style
- salutation
- date
- construct
- complimentary
- colloquialisms
- close
- address

Q10 Arrange the following words into pairs:

- neither
- could
- or
- either
- should
- of
- nor
- have

Q11 Using a dictionary if necessary, consider when you would use the following words in correspondence:

- less
- fewer
- taller
- shorter
- illegible
- ineligible
- aloud
- allowed

Q12 Read the following message:

'Hi Sue 4got 2 go 2 mtg yestday. Did u bring yr notes bc. If so cn u bring thm 2 my office l8tr!'

When might you (or someone you know) send a message like this?

a. When you are asking your line manager for some information.
b. When sending an email.
c. When sending a text via a mobile phone.

Q13 Look at the two examples below and pair the correct salutation and complimentary close together.

Salutation:

a. Dear Sir (or Dear Madam)
b. Dear Mrs Smith (or Dear Mr Smith)

Complimentary close:

a. Yours faithfully
b. Yours sincerely

A SUMMARY OF KEY POINTS

In this chapter you have learned about:

> the need to follow standard conventions for different text types with different functions;

> planning and drafting writing;

> selecting appropriate formats and styles of writing for different purposes and different readers;

> font sizes and styles appropriate to the intended audience in word-processed documents;

> identifying some errors and confusion in word usage.

REFERENCES AND FURTHER READING REFERENCES AND FURTHER READING

Websites

Access For All (2001): **www.dcsf.gov.uk/curriculum_literacy/access/**
Adult Literacy Core Curriculum, (2008): **www.dfes.gov.uk/curriculum_literacy/tree/writing/writingcomp/l2/**
Businessballs (2009): **www.businessballs.com**
Data Protection Act (1988): **www.opsi.gov.uk/Acts/Acts1998/ukpga_19980029_en_1**
Guidance to Teachers and Employers, Literacy: **www.dfes.gov.uk/curriculum_literacy/tree/writing/writingcomp/l2/**
LLUK (Sept., 2008) Evidencing Personal Skills, in Literacy and Numeracy: **www.lluk.org/documents/evidencing-personal-skills-requirements.pdf**
Minimum Core (2007): **www.lluk.org.uk/minimum_core_may_2007_3rd.pdf**
Move on (2008): **www.move-on.org.uk**

Qualifications and Curriculum Authority (2004) Communication Key Skill, QCA: **www.qca.org.uk/14-19/11-16-schools/index_s5-3-using-key-skills.htm**

Skillswise (2008): **www.bbc.co/skillswise**

Standards Verification, UK (2007): **www.standardsverificationuk.org/documents/ Evidencing_the_personal_skills_in_English_Mathematics_and_ICT_FINAL.pdf**

4
Punctuation

By the end of this chapter you should be able to:

- use punctuation to establish meaning;
- use punctuation according to accepted rules and conventions;
- use punctuation to achieve specific effects;
- punctuate sentences correctly;
- use punctuation accurately;
- use clauses, sentences and texts consistently when producing written text.

This chapter and the objectives contribute to the following Minimum Core requirements:
Part B; Personal Language Skills: Spelling and Punctuation.

This chapter also contributes towards the following LLUK standards:
AS 4, AS 7, AP 4.2, AP 4.3, CK. 3.4, CP3.4
Also relevant to the Adult Core Curriculum Ws/L2.

Key information

Using punctuation incorrectly or not using it at all can result in making the meaning of sentences and paragraphs different to what you intended.

Importantly your learners could misinterpret the message that you wish to convey if you do not use punctuation correctly when preparing handouts and presentations for your learners.

When you are writing assignments, marks are awarded or taken away depending upon how good your punctuation is. If your skill at using punctuation properly is limited, your assignment may not be coherent and you will fail or be referred.

What is punctuation?
Punctuation is all of the marks used within writing that are not either letters or numbers. Punctuation marks that are frequently used include:

- full stops, question marks, exclamation marks, commas, inverted commas, semi-colons, colons, brackets, apostrophes, hyphens and dashes.

Punctuation helps to structure your words by breaking them into sentences, clauses, phrases and paragraphs. Punctuation also includes the appropriate use of capital letters.

Punctuation that is perhaps used less frequently includes:

acute accent (á)	This is used in some languages and aids pronunciation of the word.
ampersand (&)	This is used in place of the word 'and'. In formal writing the ampersand should never replace the word 'and' except when referring to names of firms, authors or recognised partnerships, e.g. Smith & Jones Solicitors; Lancaster & Tunnicliffe Publishers.
asterisk (*)	Used when words or letters are missing. It is also used to indicate a footnote.
forward slash or oblique (/)	This is used to indicate alternative words or choices, e.g. his/hers, school/college. Also used in internet addresses.
grave accent (à)	This is used in some languages and aids pronunciation of the word.
hash (#)	Often used when referring to computer programming, or within internet addresses.

Sentences

As a teacher you may need to write lengthy letters and reports. As a trainee teacher you will certainly need to write lengthy assignments. You may also need to mark learners' work that requires amendments to their punctuation, including sentence structure.

Sentences need punctuation to determine where they stop (use of full stop) and to make appropriate breaks within them through the use of commas, colons and semi-colons.

What is a sentence?

A sentence is a group of words that make sense on their own. A sentence always has at least one verb and starts with a capital letter. A full stop, question mark or exclamation mark is used at the end of a sentence. There are simple sentences, compound sentences and multiple sentences.

A *simple sentence* contains a statement, a verb and a subject, for example:

> *The Principal was angry.*

A *compound sentence* links two statements together, for example:

> *The Principal was angry, but she still let Yvonne take the examination.*

The sentence above could be split into two simple sentences but has been joined together by a comma.

A *multiple sentence* links three or more statements together, for example:

> *The Principal was angry, but she still let Yvonne take the examination, and provided her with the appropriate equipment.*

The sentence above could be split into three sentences but has been joined by two commas.

Varying the length of sentences enriches your writing and aids the interest of the reader.

Paragraphs

Paragraphs are very important. Each paragraph should contain similar thoughts and ideas. Paragraphs should be organised so that the information is structured and the reader can follow an argument or a point of view.

When you write a piece of work always check that you have banded similar ideas together into one or more paragraphs and that differing ideas are not 'jumping' around within the same paragraph.

Moreover, paragraphs should, when possible, be linked by using connective words or phrases such as:

* furthermore;
* moreover;
* similarly;
* with consideration to the above.

Most people display paragraphs by leaving a clear line space between each one. Another way that is sometimes still used it to indent each new paragraph by five spaces. The first method is preferable.

Capital letters

A capital letter is used for the following reasons:

* at the beginning of a new sentence;
* abbreviated words and acronyms (PTLLS, CTLLS, DTLLS, LLS).

Capital letters are also used for proper nouns, including:

* *days of the week*, e.g. Monday, Tuesday;
* *months of the year,* e.g. January, February;
* *names of people*, e.g. Gloria, Shazia, Jason, Haim;
* *names of places*, e.g. London, Bristol, America, Asia;
* *names of races*, e.g. Americans, British, Asians, French;
* *names of religions*, e.g. Christians, Muslims, Jews, Buddhists;
* *salutations*, e.g. Dear Sir, Dear Madam;
* *special festivals*, e.g. Christmas, Ramadan, Passover, Diwali;
* *surnames*, e.g. Whitehurst, Keller, Kowolkosko, Ashraf;
* *titles*, e.g. Mr, Mrs, Miss, Dr.

Remember, always use capital letters for names of people and places. However, some things also need capital letters and this is where mistakes are often made. If the 'thing' is one of many, then the general rule is not to use a capital letter. So, for example, you would never use a capital letter for words like television, computers, furniture etc. If, however, the 'thing' is a one-off, then you would use a capital letter.

> **EXAMPLE**
> **Examples of words with capital letters:**
> * God, Bible, Koran, Torah, London Bridge.
>
> If you are using speech marks you start with a capital letter, for example:
>
> * She said, *"You can start a mentoring course in September"*.

Full stops

A full stop is used at the end of a sentence unless the sentence requires a question mark or an exclamation mark:

Three full stops are used to indicate an omission of words from a sentence. This is a method often used within academic and report writing when only the key points from the sentence are required, for example:

Bloom's (1956) taxonomy is still widely quoted ... even though it is dated.

Question mark

A question mark is used to ask a question and replaces the use of a full stop, for example:

When is a full stop used?

Exclamation mark

An exclamation mark is used to express a strong feeling or outburst. It is used instead of a full stop, for example:

Stop!

It is not generally good practice to use questions and exclamation marks with your assignments. It is also generally not good practice to use exclamation marks on learners' work as it could cause offence.

Comma

The comma is possibly the most used punctuation mark. The comma never has a white space preceding it and always has a white space following it. Below are examples of the most regular uses of the comma.

The listing comma

This comma is used instead of the word 'and' when a list of three or more is given, for example:

The teacher thought that Susan, David and Brian had done their homework.

The joining comma

The joining comma can cause much confusion. The joining comma joins two or more sentences together. A joining comma must be followed by a connecting word. Connecting words that can be used are *and*, *but*, *while*, *yet*, for example:

- The learners were not very motivated, *but* nevertheless continued to work.
- The teacher told their learners that assignments must be in on Monday, *and* they must ensure that they get a receipt for them.

The most important thing to remember when joining two complex sentences together is that you follow it by using one of the connecting words.

Bracketing commas
Bracketing commas are the most commonly used commas and the ones that are used the most inappropriately. A pair of bracketing commas is used to insert additional information between parts of a sentence without interrupting the flow and main meaning of the sentence, for example:

EXAMPLE
- I have marked most of the assignments, all of which have passed, and I will mark the others tomorrow.
- Last year's group had a party, a jolly good one, at the end of the academic year.
- The information is correct, thank goodness, and can now be posted out to the parents.

The important thing to note when using bracketing commas is that if the words slotted between the two commas were removed the sentence would still make complete sense, for example:

Last year's group had a party at the end of the academic year.

If the sentence does not make sense, then the commas have been used incorrectly – so either do not use them or construct your sentence differently.

Brackets
Brackets, also called parentheses or dividers, are used exactly the same as bracketing commas, for example:

The examination procedures (and there are many of them) can be found within the pack provided.

A further use for them is to include a complete sentence within them that provides information as an aside to the information outside of the brackets. If a complete sentence is included within the brackets, then the full stop is also inside the brackets, for example:

The Minimum Core represents the level of competence that teachers need to be operating at. (Information about the Minimum Core can be found on the Internet.)

Colon
The colon never has a white space preceding it but always has one following it. Some people use a colon followed by a hyphen but this is incorrect and you should never do this. The most common reason for using a colon is before a list, for example:

The refectory sold many items including: stationery, sweets, chocolates and cards.

Colons are usually preceded by a complete sentence and their use is to add some additional information to that sentence, for example:

The open day was a huge success: thanks to the learners' efforts.

Semi-colon

A semi-colon is used to join two sentences together because the two sentences are closely linked. It is often used because there is no suitable connector like 'and' or 'but' to join the sentences together, for example:

The days were passing swiftly; there was so much work to do.

The above example could easily be split into two sentences.

The days were passing swiftly. There was so much work to do.

The semi-colon can also be used for splitting up lists, within a sentence, when it is very long, for example:

I have four people to thank for my success: my partner who has always supported me; my children for caring; my parents for giving up so much for me; and my friends for always being there for me.

Hyphens and dashes

Hyphens and dashes are sometimes used incorrectly. A hyphen links two independent words together to make one word, for example:

T-shirt, co-operative, U-turn, non-verbal.

Dashes are used to show a range between numbers, dates and places, for example:

The 1970s–1980s
John O'Groats–Land's End
The course would cost £300–£400

A dash is also sometimes used instead of a full stop or comma to join two similar thoughts together. It has a white space preceding it and a white space immediately after it. However, in academic and formal writing the dash should either not be used or be used sparingly. For example:

The DTLLS course is in its second year – the CTLLS course finished months ago.

Quotation marks/inverted commas

Quotation marks, inverted commas and speech marks are the same thing. They are applied directly before and directly after direct speech. Direct speech can be stating something exactly as someone has said it (word for word) and it can also mean words taken directly from a book (i.e. being directly quoted), for example:

- *She said, 'You were late this morning'.*
- *Smith (2008) states that 'all learners should be actively engaged in the learning process'.*

Inverted commas may also be used to indicate words within sentences that need to stand out or be slightly separated from the other words, for example:

The research was interesting as the 'case' was topical and had recently been in the media.

Nowadays many people use single inverted commas rather than double inverted commas for direct speech. Both are acceptable in formal and academic writing.

HINTS AND TIPS

Quotation marks and speech marks always follow the final punctuation mark at the end of the period of direct speech, for example:

'When do we have a break for lunch?' asked Jason.

Apostrophes

Apostrophes are frequently misused. Sometimes apostrophes are used when they should not be, sometimes they are not used when they should be, and apostrophes are also often inserted incorrectly. However, apostrophes are not optional and they should always be used appropriately.

There are three reasons for using apostrophes:

- when using contracted words;
- to show possession;
- to indicate plural forms within abbreviations and numbers.

Contracted words

Contracted words are two words that have been joined together, with some letters omitted, to make one word. The apostrophe is used to indicate that some letters have been omitted. Some examples are:

can't – cannot
didn't – did not
shouldn't – should not
wouldn't – would not
don't – do not
o'clock – of the clock
'89 – 1989

HINTS AND TIPS

Its or it's

The use of 'its' or 'it's' can cause great confusion for some people. 'Its' without an apostrophe is a pronoun and 'it's' with an apostrophe is a contraction. You never put an apostrophe in 'its' if you cannot expand the word to 'it is' and the sentence would still make sense.

Examples

- *It's raining today.* It *is* raining today.
- *The fox chased its tail.* The fox chased it *is* tail – this doesn't make sense so there is no apostrophe required.

Several words are often written incorrectly, for example:

> **EXAMPLE**
>
> Your – *is a possessive adjective, e.g. Your bag is on the table.*
>
> You're – *is a contracted word for 'you are', e.g. You're late.*
>
> Whose – *refers to possession, e.g. Whose book is it?*
>
> Who's – *is a contracted word, e.g. Who's going to Tim's party?*

Possessive use of apostrophes
The possessive apostrophe is used when someone or something owns, or has possession, of something (i.e. the word requiring the apostrophe will be a noun).

The learner's work was very good. (The work belonging to/owned by the learner was very good.)

Singular words with an apostrophe
Singular apostrophes generally have the apostrophe before the 's' is added to the word, for example:

- *The boy's report was on the teacher's table. (There is one boy so the apostrophe comes before the 's'. There is one teacher so the apostrophe comes before the 's'. The boy owns/ possesses the report and the table belongs to the teacher.)*
- *The lady's pen was broken. (There is one lady so the apostrophe comes before the 's'. The lady owns/ possesses the broken pen.)*

However, if a singular word that already ends in an 's' or a double 's' ('ss') requires an apostrophe, then it is appropriate to insert the apostrophe following the 's' (or 'ss') without the need of adding a further 's', for example:

Charles' dog is a little Jack Russell, named Honey. (Charles already ends in an 's' so there is no need to add another one. However, an apostrophe is required to show ownership/possession because Charles owns a dog, a Jack Russell, named Honey.)

Plural words with an apostrophe
Plural words generally have the apostrophe after the 's', for example:

- *The learners' work was all of a good standard. (There was more than one learner who possessed/owned some work and therefore the apostrophe is placed after the 's'.)*
- *The girls' and boys' shirts were all rather dirty after they had finished their game of football. (There is more than one girl and more than one boy who own/ possess shirts and therefore the apostrophe is placed after the 's'.)*

However, if a plural word already ends in an 's' or 'ss' and requires an apostrophe then it is appropriate to insert the apostrophe following the 's' (or 'ss') without the need of adding a further 's', for example:

- *The ladies' dresses were all the same colour. (The plural word 'ladies' already ends in an 's' so there is no need to add another one. The ladies own/possess the dresses so an apostrophe is required.)*

Exceptions to the plural/singular rule generally occur when a word has already become plural before adding an 's' but the plural form does not end in an 's'. In these instances the apostrophe comes before the 's', for example:

Children's shoes, men's socks, women's clothes.

HINTS AND TIPS

Just because a word has an 's' at the end of it does not mean that it requires an apostrophe. No doubt you will have seen signs like:

Carrot's, Apple's, Pear's, Greengrocer's.

These examples are wrong. Remember, unless it is a contracted word or the word 'owns something', then you do not need an apostrophe.

Leaving out apostrophes
You should avoid using abbreviations unless they are abbreviations that are commonly used (i.e. not words that you have decided to abbreviate to save time in writing or to keep within a word count).

Currently, it is more usual for apostrophes to be left out of abbreviations and numbers, for example:

1930s
As and Bs
SATs
GCSEs

Avoiding ambiguity

Using punctuation correctly can avoid any misunderstandings within the message. You may have read emails or information from other sources that has made you laugh because of their ambiguity. More seriously you may have incorrectly acted upon information as a result of a message being ambiguous, for example:

Could you please email the following people and ask if they can provide target numbers for learners enrolling onto DTLLS and CTLLS next year before next Thursday.

The above statement could imply that some learners were enrolling onto next year's courses before next Thursday.

The above statement could also mean that the information was required before next Thursday.

If the sentence is restructured using commas, the meaning becomes clear, for example:

Could you please email the following people and ask if they can provide, before next Thursday, target numbers for learners enrolling onto DTLLS and CTLLS next year.

Abbreviations and acronyms

When using abbreviations and acronyms it is important that you maintain the same style throughout a document. That is, you should either punctuate between letters or leave punctuation out all together. Examples include:

- *Prof. or Prof (abbreviation of Professor)*
- *P.G.C.E. or PGCE (abbreviation of Post Graduate Certificate in Education)*
- *D.O.B. or DOB (abbreviation of Date of Birth)*
- *D.I.U.S. or DIUS (abbreviation of Department of Industry, Universities and Schools)*

If you use the fully punctuated method there is always a full point at the end of the abbreviation. Currently many people choose to leave out the punctuation and generally this is now accepted practice.

HINTS AND TIPS
The two words below are commonly confused abbreviations:

- i.e. – you are saying, or writing, 'that is'
- e.g. – you are saying, or writing, 'for example'

Do not confuse the two meanings.

Key questions

Now have a go at the exercises below.
These exercises are designed to help you test yourself in this topic. Some are reflective questions and thus require you to discuss your potential answers with colleagues/tutors. Some require you to use a dictionary, spell checker or other resources that will be available to you. Work through the exercises and note your answers on a separate sheet. The answers can be found at the back of the book.

Q1 Read the following paragraph and punctuate correctly.

This papers purpose is to explore concepts and policies relating to the professionalism of Further Education (F.E.) also referred to as the Lifelong Learning sector and the underpinning fundamental principles upon which the current and future initial teacher training (ITT) programmes within F.E. are and should be developed! The paper has been organised to combine relevant historical background of F.E. with current notions of what the fundamental principles are or should be within F.E Within this, content, the objectives are to, analyse and evaluate teacher training models and teaching cultures within F.E. Also given importance within the assignment are differing theories of professionalism and some - conflicting arguments relating to whether or not lecturers actually want to become professionalised? Unless otherwise stated the term 'teacher' refers to work-ing teaching staff within F.E., as does, the term lecturer Literature uses' both of these terms to mean the same thing.

Q2 Complete the exercise below. Replace each series of dots with the correct word (or words).

Two dots above each other are called a …….. whereas a dot with a comma below it is called a …….. If you want to break a sentence up without using a full stop you could use a ……….. or a pair of …………… . A ……….. joins two words together to make one differ-ent word. I think that I will scream if I see another …………. …………. at the end of a sentence where there should be a ………. …….. or a …………. …………..

- brackets
- colon
- comma
- exclamation mark
- full stop
- hyphen
- question mark
- semi-colon

Q3 Look at the following sentences and insert an apostrophe as appropriate:
For 'learner' (2 and 10) assume there is a group of learners.

1. The cats ball had burst.
2. The learners work had been marked.
3. The door was coming off its hinge.
4. When I was teaching this afternoon I noticed that the childrens chairs had been rearranged.
5. My work was at my sisters house.
6. Its a good thing that the learners arrived at their class on time.
7. All of the girls mothers had attended the event.
8. The babies bottles were all washed.
9. The babys rattles were on the floor.
10. The learners homework was handed in on time.

Q4 Choose the right word from within the brackets:

1. The (eyes, eye's, eyes') were the darkest I had ever seen.
2. The (childrens', children's, childrens) books were in the cupboard.
3. Yesterday the (greengrocers, greengrocer's, greengrocers') was closed. This was a pity because I wanted some (carrots, carrot's, carrots') for my (son's, sons, sons') tea.

Choose one correct answer from each of the questions below.

Q5 1. A simple sentence must contain:
   a) a clause
   b) a verb
   c) an object

2. A joining comma can be followed by the word:
   a) and
   b) rather
   c) similarly
3. A capital letter is used:
   a) for common nouns
   b) for proper nouns
   c) for words following an apostrophe

Q6 Correct with the following abbreviations or acronyms?

1. LLUk
2. ie.
3. e.g
4. PG.CE
5. D.I.U.S

Q7 Which of the following words could be joined using a hyphen?

co opt   winter festival
cooperative   ante natal
man made   anti war
part time   pro European
summer time   lunch time
T shirt   top marks

Q8 Which of the following words should have an apostrophe?

cant   hers
hours   ours
theirs   theres
whos   whose
yours   youre

Q9 Write a short paragraph using the following punctuation marks:

- question mark
- ampersand
- full stop
- colon
- hyphen
- brackets
- comma
- dash
- apostrophe

Q10 Re-write the following phrases by removing the words 'belonging to' and inserting an apostrophe in the appropriate place:

1. The theatre tickets belonging to Denry.
2. The blue dresses belonging to the ladies.
3. The craft items belonging to children.
4. The timetable belonging to the year.
5. The equipment belonging to the lecturers.

A SUMMARY OF KEY POINTS

In this chapter you have learned about:

> **using punctuation to establish meaning;**

> **using punctuation according to accepted rules and conventions;**

> **using punctuation to achieve specific effects;**

> **punctuating sentences correctly;**

> **using punctuation accurately;**

> **using clauses, sentences and texts.**

REFERENCES AND FURTHER READING REFERENCES AND FURTHER READING

Department for Education and Skills (2001) *Adult ESOL Core Curriculum*. London: DfES
Department for Education and Skills (2001) *Pre-Entry Curriculum Framework*. London: DfES
Department for Education and Skills (2002) *Introducing Access for All*. London: DfES

Websites
Access For All (2001); **www.dcsf.gov.uk/curriculum_literacy/access/**
Adult Literacy Core Curriculum (2008): **www.dfes.gov.uk/curriculum_literacy/tree/ writing/writingcomp/l2/**
Guidance to Teachers and Employers Literacy (2008):
    www.dfes.gov.uk/curriculum_literacy/tree/writing/writingcomp/l2/
LLUK (Sept. 2008) Evidencing Personal Skills in Literacy and Numeracy:
    www.lluk.org/documents/evidencing-personal-skills-requirements.pdf
Minimum Core (2007): **www.lluk.org.uk/minimum_core_may_2007_3rd.pdf**
Move on (2008): **www.move-on.org.uk**
National Qualification Framework (2009): **www.direct.gov.uk/en/EducationAndLearning/ QualificationsExplained/DG_10039017**
Qualification Improvement Agency Excellence Gateway (2008): **www.excellence.qui.org.uk**
Qualifications and Curriculum Authority (2000) National Basic Skills Standards, QCA:
    www.qca.org.uk/14-19/qualifications/116_main-qualifications-gp.htm
Skillswise: **www.bbc.co/skillswise**
www.lluk.org/documents/evidencing-personal-skills-requirements.pdf

5
Spelling

By the end of this chapter you should be able to:

- apply a range of methods to help you to remember how to spell certain words;
- look up words using a dictionary or electronic spell checker;
- give examples of words that sound the same (homophones);
- identify root words;
- create different words from root words using prefixes and suffixes;
- split polysyllabic words as an aid to spelling them correctly.

This chapter and the objectives contribute to the Minimum Core requirements:
Part B; Personal Language Skills: Spelling.

This chapter also contributes towards the following LLUK standards:
AS 4, AS 7, AP 4.2, AP 4.3, AP7.1, AP7.2, AP7.3, BP3.1, BP3.3, CK3.4, CP3.4.
Also relevant to the Adult Core Curriculum Ww/L2.

Key information

Most, if not all, of us make spelling mistakes. This can be because we have rushed a piece of work and not proofread it or because we do not know how to spell certain words.

Many teachers will be able to provide anecdotal comments about mistakes on handouts or writing something on the board and not being able to remember how to spell a word. However, poor spelling can have an effect on a teacher's confidence and the teaching and learning strategies that they employ.

Vowels and consonants

The alphabet, and therefore words, consists of vowels and consonants. There are five vowels:

a, e, i, o, u.

The rest of the alphabet letters are called consonants.

Proofreading

All work should be proofread. As a teacher your writing is an extension of your professionalism and it is important that you create a good impression.

Computer programs have spell check facilities. It is advisable that you always make use of this facility. However, be mindful of the fact that some words and spellings are not recognised by the spell check facility and furthermore often have the American way of spelling a word rather than the English way. If in doubt it is advisable to use a good dictionary. If possible, it is very useful to ask someone else to read your work.

Root words

Root words are complete words with nothing added at the beginning (prefix) and nothing added at the end (suffix). For example:

sincere, faithful, true, locate, clear, standard, fortune.

New words can be made from root words and this is often when spelling mistakes can be made.

Prefixes

Prefixes are added to the beginning of a root word to change the meaning of it. Common examples of prefixes are 'mis' and 'sub', for example:

If you add the prefix 'mis' to the root word 'fortune' the word becomes 'misfortune'.
If you add the prefix 'sub' to the root word 'standard' the word becomes 'substandard'.

HINTS AND TIPS
A prefix never alters the spelling of the root word.

Suffixes

Suffixes are added at the end of a root word to change the meaning of it. Common examples of suffixes are 'ed' and 'ly', for example:

If the root word is 'faithful' and you add the suffix 'ly' the word becomes 'faithfully'.

If the root word is 'locate' and you add the suffix 'ed' the word becomes 'located'.

Prefix – root – suffix

Some root words have a prefix and a suffix attached to them, for example:

If you add the prefix 'dis' to the root word 'regard' and then add the suffix 'ed' the word becomes 'disregarded'.

Words containing the suffix '-ly'

A mistake some people make is to add the suffix '-ley' when they should add '-ly'. Generally, you should spell the root word in full and then add '-ly', for example:

'Faithfully' is often spelt incorrectly as 'faithfuley'.
'Sincerely' is often spelt incorrectly as sincereley'.

Dropping an 'e'

If a root word ends in a vowel and the suffix starts with a vowel, then generally the vowel is removed from the root word before the suffix is attached:

The root word 'love' has the 'e' removed before adding the suffix '-ing' to make the word 'loving'.

The root word 'excite' has the 'e' removed before adding the suffix '-able' to make 'excitable'.

Can you think of any more?

One baby, two babies...
The general rule here is to remove the 'e' from the end of the singular word and add the suffix 'ies', for example:

   lady – ladies
   baby – babies

Where the word ends in 'ey' the plural simply adds an 's' for example: *donkey, donkeys*.

Words ending in '-cede', '-ceed' or '-sede'
Nearly all words that end with the sound of 'seed' are spelt '-cede'. Exceptions to this rule include exceed, succeed and proceed.

Rarely would words end in '-sede', so unless you are spelling 'supersede' you will probably never use it.

- prefixes and suffixes can help you to understand the meaning of words.
- auto – means self, e.g. automatic, autocorrect.
- dis – means not, e.g. disagree, disappear, disappoint.
- mis – means the absence of something, e.g. misfortune, misplace.
- ology – means the study of something, e.g. sociology, psychology.
- phone – means a sound, e.g. telephone, homophone.
- ware – means something manufactured, e.g. earthenware, silverware.

Beware of double consonants
Whether certain words include double consonants or not can be problematic even for good spellers. There is no specific rule to knowing which words have a double consonant and which do not.

Some words that are often incorrectly spelt include:

accommodation	abbreviate	assess	committed
correspondence	curriculum	embarrass	excellent
efficient	effective	grammatical	miscellaneous
occurred	omitted	opportunity	possess
questionnaire	recommend	succeed	success

Homophones
'Homo' means the 'same as' and 'phone' means 'sound' so homophone means two or more words that sound the same, for example:

- *fair – fare – fayre*
- *pair – pear – pare*
- *red – read*
- *there – their*
- *to – two – too*

- *wait – weight*
- *way – weigh*
- *wear – where – ware*
- *hair – hare*
- *cue – queue*

Verbs and nouns

Some words sound the same (or similar) but are spelt differently depending upon whether they are a verb or a noun.

When to use 'ie' and when to use 'ei'

You will probably have heard the rule 'i before e except after c'.

Generally this is a good rule to follow. However, the rule tends to apply only to those words that have an 'ee' sound, for example:

believe, relieve, shield.

Words that have an 'ee' sound preceded by the letter 'c' are usually spelt 'ei'; for example:

deceive, receive, perceive.

Words that do not have an 'ee' sound (usually they have an 'ay' sound) are usually formed with 'ei', for example:

weight, neighbour, beige.

Polysyllabic words

A syllable is a unit of speech that a person would interpret as a single sound. Therefore, polysyllabic words have more than one unit of speech and more than one sound, for example:

dif-fer-ent, re-mem-ber, to-mor-row.

When spelling words it may sometimes be useful to break down the words into single syllables (sounds) and then join them together, for example:

cur-ric-u-lum, card-board, gov-ern-ment.

Some general rules

Some words are easily confused and other words, because they sound the same (homophones), are used inappropriately. Some examples are:

Alright – although this word is often used and accepted by some, it is incorrect and you should always use 'all right'.

All ready – means prepared.
Already – means an action previously done.

Ante – means before something.
Anti – means against something.

Complement – means to complete something.
Compliment – means to express praise.

Stationery – means paper, envelopes, etc.
Stationary – means to be still, not moving.

> **HINTS AND TIPS**
>
> There is no such word as 'thankyou' in the English language. You should always use 'thank you'.
>
> There is no such word as 'alot' in the English language. You should always use 'a lot', although it is a term that is best not used at all.

Dictionaries, electronic spell checkers

Remember that the spell-checker available on the computer that you use will be very helpful but it is not always right. You sometimes need to know the meaning of the word to ensure that the right word is used; a dictionary is very good for this, and you will notice that many people who you consider to be good at spelling often reach for the dictionary.

A good dictionary is also very useful at providing information on how to pronounce words and the variations of the spellings of some words.

Of course if you do not know the beginning letters of a word (for example, words with a silent 'k' or silent 'p'), then a dictionary may not be of use. In such cases think of the meaning of the word and look in a thesaurus for a word that is similar to the word you want. You may find the word you want listed by the alternative word.

Key questions

Now have a go at the exercises.

These exercises are designed to help you test yourself in this topic. Some are reflective questions and thus require you to discuss your potential answers with colleagues/tutors. Some require you to use a dictionary, spell checker or other resources that will be available to you. Work through the exercises and note your answers on a separate sheet. The answers can be found at the back of the book.

Q1 Look at the words in the list below and decide which words are spelt correctly and which words are incorrect. All of the words are ones that are often used within written communication (use a dictionary or electronic spell-checker to help you if necessary).

absence	accept	accommodation	acheive
alright	bureucracy	calender	collegue
competent	course	curricullum	conscientius
definitley	eligible	grammer	liase
maintainence	mandatory	naughty	occurance
obscure	obselete	ordinery	office
programme	presence	possibly	questionnaire
qualitative	quantative	rhyme	separatley
sincerley	syllabus	system	sinthesis
temporarirly	taught	thorou	test
withold	winner	whether	zenophobia

Q2 Add a suffix, profix or both to the words below (use a dictionary or electronic spell-checker to help you if necessary).

Prefix	Root	Suffix	Prefix	Root	Suffix
	relate			honest	
	joint			regard	
	led			behave	
	proportionate			agree	
	fortune			use	

Q3 Read the following sentences and choose one word from within the bracket that you think is the right word (use a dictionary or electronic spell-checker to help you if necessary).

1. The learners were allowed (brakes, breaks) every three hours.
2. The teacher's (accommodation, acommodation) was not of the standard expected.
3. The (Principle, Principal) sent a letter to all staff about their working hours.
4. When we went to the college the learners had (already, all ready) prepared for our visit.
5. Yesterday the class was (canceled, cancelled) due to the snow.
6. (Unfortunatley, unfortunately) the teacher did not turn up for his class.
7. Risk assessment and Health and Safety are now very (rigerous, rigorous) processes.
8. The teacher gave me good (advice, advise) on how to complete my assignment.

9. Several (statements, statments) were made about the bullying incident. Each one seemed to (superceed, supercede, supersede) the previous one.
10. There was an uproar when one teacher was given an additional day (of, off). The teachers (thaught, thought) that they should have an extra day (two, to, too)

Q4 *Look at the questions below and circle the correct answer (use a dictionary or electronic spell-checker to help you if necessary).*

1. Which word means to have the correct answer?
   a) wright
   b) right
2. Which word is a preposition?
   a) to
   b) two
   c) too
3. Which word means more than one?
   a) pear
   b) pair
4. Which word means to be fed up?
   a) bored
   b) board
5. Which word means to use your eyesight?
   a) sea
   b) see

Q5 Split the polysyllabic words in the table into single syllables. The first one is done as an example.

remainder	re-main-der	discipline
teacher		successful
assignment		telephone
classroom		temperature
resource		excellent

Q6 First, think of three words that end in the following suffixes, and second, use a dictionary to check your answers:

-able	-ology
-ful	-phone
-ible	-tion
-less	-naut
-ly	-ware
-ment	

Q7 Provide a meaning for the following words; use a dictionary to check your answers:

annotate
bureaucracy
esoteric
incessant
notion
nuance
phenomenon

Q8 Provide the plural of the singular words listed below:

1. cotton
2. criterion
3. curriculum
4. formula
5. human
6. injury
7. louse
8. wheat

Q9 Use a thesaurus to look up different meanings for the following words; ensure that you note the spelling of the words:

distinctive	regimented
idea	stralghtforward
peculiar	summary

Q10 What is the difference between the following words? (use a dictionary to check your answers):

affect and effect

allusion and illusion

compliment and complement

dependent and dependant

discreet and discrete

learned and learnt

leased and least

Q11 What are the meanings of the following prefixes and suffixes? (use a dictionary to find the answers if necessary):

Prefix	meaning	Suffix	meaning
ante		able	
ex		ish	
mono		ed	
anti		less	
poly		ment	
hyper		ness	

A SUMMARY OF KEY POINTS

In this chapter you have learned about:

> methods to help you to remember how to spell certain words;

> dictionaries or electronic spell-checkers;

> homophones;

> root words;

> prefixes and suffixes;

> polysyllabic words.

REFERENCES AND FURTHER READING REFERENCES AND FURTHER READING

Department for Education and Skills (2001) *Adult ESOL Core Curriculum*. London: DfES
Department for Education and Skills (2001) *Pre-Entry Curriculum Framework*. London: DfES
Department for Education and Skills (2002) *Introducing Access for All*. London: DfES

Websites
Access For All (2001): **www.dcsf.gov.uk/curriculum_literacy/access/**
Adult Literacy Core Curriculum (2008): **www.dfes.gov.uk/curriculum_literacy/tree/writing/writingcomp/l2/**
Guidance to Teachers and Employers' Literacy: **www.dfes.gov.uk/curriculum_literacy/tree/writing/writingcomp/l2/**
LLUK (Sept. 2008) Evidencing Personal Skills in Literacy and Numeracy: **www.lluk.org/documents/evidencing-personal-skills-requirements.pdf**
Minimum Core (2007): **www.lluk.org.uk/minimum_core_may_2007_3rd.pdf**
Move on (2008): **www.move-on.org.uk**
National Qualification Framework (2008): **www.readingroom.lsc.gov.uk/lsc/WestMidlands/The_National_Qualifications_Framework_2008.pdf**
Qualification Improvement Agency Excellence Gateway (2008): **www.excellence.qia.org.uk/**
Qualifications and Curriculum Authority (2000): National Basic Skills Standards, QCA: **www.qca.org.uk/14-19/qualifications/116_main-qualifications-gp.htm**
Skillswise (2008): **www.bbc.co/skillswisewww.direct.gov.uk/en/EducationAndLearning/QualificationsExplained/DG_**

6
Speaking and listening

By the end of this chapter you should be able to:

- recognise how to use different communication techniques to help convey meaning and to enhance the delivery and accessibility of the message;
- appreciate the impact that language, style and tone can have when speaking;
- recall appropriate techniques to reinforce oral communication, check how well the information is received and support the understanding of those listening;
- recognise the importance of appropriate language to support learners and to communicate appropriately with others;
- provide examples of what it means to listen attentively and to respond sensitively to contributions made by others.

This chapter and the objectives contribute to the following Minimum Core requirements: Part B; Personal Language Skills: Speaking and Listening.

This chapter contributes towards the following LLUK standards: **AS4, AS5, AS7, AP5.2, BP3.1, BP3.2, BP3.4, CP3.4.** Also relevant to the Adult Core Curriculum SLc/L2.

Key information

Within your role as an F.E. teacher you will be required to engage and communicate verbally and to be able to listen attentively. Exceptions to this could include those who choose, or those who need, to communicate through some other medium, for example using sign language.

Most social relationships, including those made within your working environment, are dependent upon speaking and listening. Furthermore, your learners' development in the subject that they are being taught and also in their use of vocabulary and presentation skills is crucially linked to your ability to speak at a level that aids their understanding and also your ability to listen to their responses. Learning is very much dependent upon the use and effectiveness of speaking (oral) and listening (aural) skills.

It is quite likely that you will spend more time speaking and listening than you will using any of the other of the personal skills in literacy (i.e. reading and writing). It is a skill, however, that you were not necessarily explicitly taught when you were at school. You will have developed your speaking and listening skills over many years and through a variety of social learning situations and interactions. Some of these may have been useful in your skill-building, confidence and competence at speaking and listening while others may have been more detrimental than helpful. For example, you may have learned to interject rather than to interrupt, or you may have learned to speak with clarity of tone rather than too quietly or too loudly.

Ask yourself the following questions:

Do you forget the main points of messages?

Do people ask you to repeat what you are saying?

Do you lose concentration when people are speaking to you?

Do you interrupt others when they are speaking?

Do you think before you speak?

Do you sometimes become defensive or angry when speaking?

Do you speak in a monotone voice?

If you have answered 'yes' to any of the above questions, then you may need to develop your speaking and listening skills.

Who's the audience?

Recognise how to use different communication techniques to help convey meaning and to enhance the delivery and accessibility of the message

Speaking and listening are modes of communication. Whether you speak formally or informally and how well you listen can be very much dependent upon your audience and your purpose.

Your audience might include:

- your line manager;
- colleagues;
- learners;
- senior management;
- parents;
- external agencies;
- external examiners;
- your teacher.

Your purpose might include to:

- inform;
- report;
- complain;
- advise;
- present;
- ask questions;
- teach;
- request;
- discuss;
- liaise.

It is quite possible and most likely that to each different audience and for each different purpose you will alter, to varying degrees, your tone, intonation and the language that you use.

HINTS AND TIPS
Think before you speak.

You cannot retract words once spoken.

Adapting to your audience

You need to consider how to vary the level of formality according to your audience and purpose and also to adapt your delivery according to the level, needs and prior knowledge of your audience.

To retain the interest of your audience, it is necessary to know how to pitch you tone and the language that you use. You need to vary the formality of your speaking according to the level, needs and prior knowledge of your audience.

Your pitch and tone express the importance and meaning of the words that you are speaking, for example 'you were late' could be said in an angry and annoyed tone or it could be said in an amazed tone (perhaps because the person is never late or because of the importance of the event).

When teaching or giving a presentation it is quite important to change the tone of your voice at times to aid interest. If you are enthused or excited about something you may notice that your tone becomes a little more high-pitched than when speaking with a normal tone. Lowering your tone and speaking slowly demonstrate authority and assertiveness. Similarly, when we ask a question it is usual for us to raise our pitch.

Many of us speak too quickly, particularly when we are nervous. It takes practice to slow down one's speech. If you do have a tendency to speak too quickly, then it may be useful for you to practise pausing between words more often than you currently do. If you are not pronouncing all of your words, and if your words are running into one another, then you are probably speaking too quickly.

HINTS AND TIPS

When speaking make sure that your sentences are of differing lengths. Variation enriches your message and provides your own unique nuances to what you are saying.

When you are planning a presentation or a teaching session, consider what language your audience will already be familiar with and how professional or friendly you need to be with them. In the classroom you are the leader and therefore your voice, tone and language used should reflect this. You can do this by being assertive (not aggressive) and by using an active voice rather than a passive voice. When you use *the active voice*, it is the subject that does the acting, while when *the passive voice* is used, the subject is acted upon. For example:

EXAMPLE

Active voice:

- I taught Stephen (the subject 'I' has performed the action).

Passive voice:

- Stephen was taught by me (Stephen becomes the subject who has been acted upon).

While both sentences are correct, it is good practice to use the active voice.

If you are presenting information to an audience or speaking at a parents' evening you need to be friendly but demonstrate respect through politeness and the use of semi-formal language. You also need to ensure that you are neither patronising nor using language that your audience does not understand.

The importance of appropriate language

When speaking to your learners you will probably use semi-formal language. This is language that uses some cliches, idioms and colloquialisms. Over-use of these, though, could confuse your learners. You should avoid being too informal when speaking, and this includes using inappropriate words that may be seen to be politically incorrect, or swear-words or words considered to be blasphemous by some sectors of the community. Being too formal could make your lesson seem staid and boring to the learners, whereas speaking too informally could make you appear over-friendly with the learners.

Idioms, colloquialism and clichés

A cliché is a much-used, and often metaphoric, phrase or expression and can become so over-used that it can irritate the listener. Examples of clichés include:

- *Vote with your feet.*
- *What goes around comes around.*
- *Always look on the bright side of life.*
- *Every cloud has a silver lining.*
- *As plain as black and white.*
- *Live and let live.*

An idiom is a phrase or expression that cannot be taken literally. Examples of idioms include:

- *Don't shoot the messenger.*
- *A frog in my throat.*
- *Kick the bucket.*
- *Break a leg.*
- *Like a bull in a china shop.*

Colloquialisms are words or sometimes phrases that should only be used when speaking informally, and even then it is good practice not to get into a habit of using them to avoid making the error of using them when speaking more formally with a different audience. Colloquialisms and the use of slang are closely related. Examples of colloquialisms include:

- *Dunno (do not know).*
- *Duck (term of endearment).*
- *Catch you later (goodbye).*
- *Catching flies (mouth open).*
- *Lead you up the garden path (mislead you).*

When speaking you need to express yourself clearly. This includes consideration and use of language that your audience can understand and respond to.

For example, your learners may not have as wide a vocabulary as you have and they may not understand what you are saying if you use words that they have not heard before. It is therefore useful to explain any words that you use that they may not understand. These could include technical words, for which you could also provide your learners with a glossary of terms, or words used and introduced through natural occurrence.

If you teach learners who are quite young, for example the 14–19 age range, they may not understand some of the words that you use if these words are no longer in everyday use. For example, if you asked a 14-year-old to switch off their wireless it is quite possible that they would have no idea what you meant. You would need to know that it was, for example, their MP4 player that they needed to switch off. In the first instance by using a term that a learner would possibly not understand, you would be making the message inaccessible. In the second instance the learner would understand quite clearly what instruction you were giving.

When you are speaking to parents or members of the public who may not be familiar with educational terms, it is important that you explain, without patronising, any words or terms that are required for clarification of meaning. An example of this would be words or phrasing like 'portfolio building', 'internal moderator', 'functional or key skills'.

Analogies, similes and metaphors

When teaching you will probably use a range of analogies to link new information to information that the learners may all ready have. An analogy therefore draws a parallel between different ideas. A simile is a figure of speech that states that something is like another thing. A simile usually contains the word 'as' or 'like', for example:

- *Clean as a whistle.*
- *Quiet as a mouse.*
- *Good as gold.*

A metaphor is also a figure of speech and is used to create an image of something, usually to aid understanding. Metaphors usually contain the word 'is', for example:

- *Her desk is a tip.*
- *It is raining cats and dogs.*

Presenting information

Presenting information can use all of your communication skills. Your written, verbal and non-verbal skills will probably be used, as will your ability to read fluently.

When giving a presentation you need to speak clearly and use pace, tone and intonation that motivates and enthuses your audience. Change your tone and pace because a monotone presentation will soon have your audience leaving, losing concentration or even falling asleep.

> **HINTS AND TIPS**
> Never include information that you do not understand.

Ensure that you have prepared your presentation and that it has a sequence and structure. Hopping from one topic to another will make the message less accessible and more difficult to follow. Make connections with different strands of your presentation and, wherever possible, provide an example that the audience can understand. To do this you need to consider the likely experiences that your audience have had and then consider how you can illustrate some of your message through these experiences. You also need to consider the use of analogies and real life examples that will help to illustrate the meaning within your message. The audience will then be able to construct your new message to knowledge that they already have.

The above technique applies equally when presenting or speaking with your learners in a classroom and to other people.

When you are teaching or giving a presentation do you:

- state your objectives using specific, measurable, attainable, realistic, timed (SMART) objectives?
- recap on the objectives at the end of the lesson or presentation?
- write key words on the board or give out a glossary of words that learners may not have heard before or may not understand?
- repeat any newly introduced words throughout the lesson or presentation to aid understanding?
- use examples and analogies that the learners will understand (i.e. will have experience of)?
- check out the learners' understanding by asking 'what', 'why' and 'how' questions?
- differentiate in your use of questioning, asking open, closed and nominated questions?
- try to chunk information into manageable parts to avoid the learners being exposed to information overload?

Choosing your words carefully

Some people seem to like the sound of their own voice. Some people also seem to think that they can impress others by the use of flowery or very elongated sentences when they are speaking. Some people do, of course, speak very eloquently and have a flair for flowery language and long sentences. However, if you are not one of those people it is advisable to give consideration to the audience and to adopt the KISS (keep it short and simple) approach and use language that gets the message or information across without any confusion. For example:

EXAMPLE

The domestic science technicians need a precondition in writing that at no times whatsoever will a request by anyone be made to them that they must use a peroxide liquid.

This could be said much more simply:

The cleaners don't want to use bleach.

Sounds the same?

Some people have a good range of vocabulary while others do not. It is good practice to continually introduce new words to your list of vocabulary, but it is crucial that you fully understand the meaning of the word and/or that you can pronounce the word correctly. Failure to do either of these can make you look incompetent or foolish. Importantly, your learners may mirror your language and they too will use words incorrectly.

Examples of words used incorrectly include:

- formerly – when you mean formally;
- brought – when you mean bought;
- affect – when you mean effect;
- biannual – when you mean biennial.

Using words for the first time

While you are studying on your teacher training course you will probably be confronted with a plethora of acronyms, many of which you will begin to use yourself when speaking to colleagues or others within FE. You will also probably hear your tutor use unfamiliar words. When a new word or an acronym has been used for the first time and the meaning has not been explained to you, have you ever stopped listening to your tutor while you are trying to work out what the acronyms or new words stand for? When you are teaching your learners may do the same (i.e. they stop listening and try to work out what the acronym or word means). This detracts from their learning experience.

In the classroom or when speaking with your learners do you:

- use appropriate words that they are able to understand while also trying to encourage them to develop their vocabulary?
- check out that they have understood?
- avoid swearing and blaspheming?
- avoid the use of slang, unfamiliar jargon and colloquialisms?
- speak in a tone and use intonations that support the verbal message?

It can be very useful to learners to have a glossary of the terms that are used, or going to be used, throughout the course or topic. Furthermore, an essential part of teaching is to embed functional skills within your planning. One way that you can do this is to consider during the planning process any new words or acronyms that you are going to introduce during the lesson. Make a note of these on your plan, and then when you use them for the first time in the classroom ensure that you explain what they mean.

Listening

Most of us are so busy that we sometimes forget to listen properly. Have you ever been asked to do something by someone at the place where you work, maybe to cover a class? If so, have you ever then tried to recall what it was that they were asking you and realised that because you were so busy you had not listened properly and had not understood fully what it was they were asking? You then have to contact the person, which takes up more of your time, and also makes the other person realise that you were not listening to them.

Active listening

Active listening is when you are concentrating on what the other person is saying to you. You want to hear and to understand their message. You may interject and ask questions to clarify what is being said.

Passive listening

Passive listening is when you are not concentrating on what the other person is saying to you. This could be because you are thinking of what you are going to say or because you are not interested in what is being said.

The process of listening

Listening is not the same as being quiet while someone else speaks. It is an active process. You need to hear the words that are being spoken, assimilate the words and, if necessary, construct an appropriate reply or use non-verbal communication (NVC, i.e. body language) that informs the speaker that you are listening to them and that you understand what they are saying. Being able to transmit and receive information or messages effectively are of equal importance.

When listening to someone it is important to provide feedback to them to demonstrate our understanding or to clarify any points that have not been understood. Feedback, which is a much-used term within teaching and learning, means that we are 'feeding back' some information in response to what the speaker has been saying. (Feedback is also a term that is commonly used when assessing learners, i.e. written or verbal feedback.)

When we are the receivers (listeners) of the transmitted (spoken) message or information we can subconsciously indicate how interested we are in what is being said by our actions. For instance, how often have you noticed someone yawn or look at their watch when you are speaking to them? Or how often have you found yourself looking at your watch when someone is speaking to you? Do your learners look at you when you are speaking, or are they staring out of the window? These NVC signs all suggest that a person is not actively listening.

Active listening is when you demonstrate clearly to someone that you are hearing what they have said. You may, for example, mirror their body language. This may include moving the top part of your body forward when sitting in your chair if they are doing the same. It may mean mirroring their smile or their frown. It will probably include nodding your head and it should definitely include eye contact – but not staring. It may also include the occasional comments such as 'yes', 'no', 'right' and 'OK'. Singular words or very short phrases provide an indication that you are following what is being said.

A poor habit to develop when listening is that of interrupting the speaker. Interrupting someone should not be confused with interjecting with someone. Interrupting can be perceived by the speaker as devaluing their message or considering yourself more important than they are. This negative impact is increased if the interruption does not relate to what the speaker is saying (or if the interruption abruptly brings an end to what the speaker was saying).

An interjection is when you wait for the right moment to speak. You have made eye contact with the speaker and from your facial expression or your body language they note that you want to speak and provide a pause in what they are saying to allow you to add your thoughts to the conversation. Interjection provides enrichment to the communication process, whereas interruption devalues the communication process.

HINTS AND TIPS

Do not use your computer (i.e. email) when someone is speaking. For example, if you see an email flash up or beep, do not be tempted to click on it. You will give the person speaking to you a very negative value message.

It is important that you demonstrate active listening skills to your learners at all times. Make eye contact with them, nod your head, smile etc. If a learner is speaking for too long, try to wait for a pause rather than stopping them in mid-sentence, and always thank them for their contribution. If they do not feel valued, or if they are made to feel awkward because they have been speaking for too long, they may become less willing or confident to speak in subsequent lessons.

HINTS AND TIPS

When asking learners questions do not be tempted to rescue them too quickly if they do not answer immediately. The silence between asking the question and receiving the answer can seem a long time, but learners need time to think about the question and formulate an answer to it. Of course it is also important that you do not leave it too long before moving on. Get the balance right.

Barriers to effective listening

There are many things that can stop us from listening to someone speaking, such as:

- tiredness;
- thinking that the speaker will be boring;
- lack of interest (perceived or real) in the subject;
- noise (mobile phones, eating in class, movement);
- jargon or information overload;
- the speaker not talking at the same level of understanding as the listener (i.e. above or below the listener's level of understanding);
- lack of sufficient comfort breaks when teaching sessions are quite long;
- distractions, including looking at something else that is happening, thinking of something else, listening to others within the vicinity.

An important point to consider is how long you speak for and how long your learners have had to listen to you. It is quite well documented that lecturing is not a particularly good teaching method to use to engage learners in their learning process (practical activities are at the top of the list for this). If you speak for more than 20 minutes then you will most likely see your learners' listening skills deteriorate, some might even go to sleep.

When preparing for a class, if possible remove distractions that might create a barrier to you or your learners' listening (i.e. shut windows if there is likely to be any noise outside, or ensure that you shut the door to lessen any distractions from the corridor).

If you are listening to your learners it is often a good idea to recap what they have said. This confirms to them that you have listened and understand what they are saying and it provides other learners with an opportunity to hear the message from both their peer and from you.

It is important that when you have finished speaking to a group of learners that you avoid saying: *'Does that make sense?'*

Learners are unlikely to say that they do not understand what you have been talking about, so you need to ask them questions to ascertain that learning has taken place. If Ofsted observe you, they will note how often you check out your learners' learning – one method of doing this is to ask many questions, particularly following a short presentation or lecture.

Finally, if you like to doodle or to make notes when you are listening to someone, then providing you still demonstrate to the speaker that you are listening there is no reason why you should not continue with this practice. You may, for example, interject and ask the occasional question or ask for an explanation about something that has been commented upon. Likewise your learners may doodle or make notes – so do not automatically think that they are not listening. Check out their NVC to see how attentive they are and, if necessary, ask them questions to confirm that they are concentrating on the message being given to them.

HINTS AND TIPS

Do not interrupt someone when they are speaking. If you do interject, ensure that you bring the topic back to where the speaker left off. You can do this by reiterating the last sentence that they had said prior to the interjection.

Do not speak to someone else when someone is talking to you. For example, if a learner is talking to you and another teacher walks by, do not speak to the teacher when the learner is speaking to you. Doing so would give the learner the impression that they were not valued, and this could affect their learning experience.

Key questions

Now have a go at the exercises.

These exercises are designed to help you test yourself in this topic. Some are reflective questions and thus require you to discuss your potential answers with colleagues/tutors. Some require you to use a dictionary, spell checker or other resources that will be available to you. Work through the exercises and note your answers on a separate sheet. The answers can be found at the back of the book.

Q1 Think of an alternative word to those given below (you can use a thesaurus if necessary):

eclectic	bureaucracy
esoteric	aforesaid
hyperbole	notion
tweaking	portfolio
24/7	could've
articulate	relational
chill-out	courting
sparky	

Q2 Look at the acronyms in the list below and write their meaning in full:

1. ATLS
2. CTLLS
3. DIUS
4. DTLLS
5. IfL
6. LLUK
7. NEET
8. NVC
9. PTLLS
10. QIA
11. QTLS
12. SEN

Q3 Decide which of the following are clichés, colloquialisms or idioms:

	Idiom	Cliché	Colloquialism
Drop in the ocean			
Naff			
Dab hand			
Nest egg			
Stretch the truth			
Barbie			
Actions speak louder than words			
As exciting as watching paint dry			
A piece of cake			
Billy no mates			
Ivory tower			
Tickled pink			

Q4 Consider the following scenario:
You have a class group of 30 learners. They are aged between 30 and 65. They attend class one evening a week for computer skills. They like to talk while they work and you allow them to do this. However, some learners have started to talk while you are trying to speak to the class. These tend to be the more able learners who do not necessarily need to listen, but their talking disrupts the class and creates a barrier to other learners being able to listen to you.

What action, if any, would you take to improve the situation?

Q5 How could you rephrase the following statement if you were teaching a group of learners aged 16–18?

The phenomenon was not new to all learners. The notion of engaging oneself in reflective practice to aid understanding of positionality was not unique.

Q6 Write down at least three metaphors and at least three similes.

Q7 What do the following statements mean?

1. That is slander.
2. I vehemently refute the statement.
3. I am somewhat reticent about it.
4. They are an anathema.
5. They were both admonished.

Q8 Select the correct pronoun from the pair in brackets:

1. The teacher was speaking to (I/me).
2. Leslie came to the college and met (I/me) for the first time.
3. Can (she/her) come with (I/me) on the expedition?
4. (He/Him) went to the lecture theatre to meet (them/they) and (we/us).
5. (Us/Our) dinner was ready when we arrived home.

A SUMMARY OF KEY POINTS

In this chapter you have learned about:

> using different communication techniques to help convey meaning and to enhance the delivery and accessibility of the message;

> the impact that language, style and tone can have when speaking;

> techniques to reinforce oral communication, to check how well the information is received and to support the understanding of those listening;

> the importance of appropriate language to support learners and to communicate appropriately with others;

> what it means to listen attentively and to respond sensitively to contributions made by others.

REFERENCES AND FURTHER READING REFERENCES AND FURTHER READING

Gravells A (2007) *Preparing to Teach in the Lifelong Learning Sector*. Exeter: Learning Matters.
Gravells A (2009) *Principles and Practice of Assessment in the Lifelong Learning Sector*. Exeter: Learning Matters.
Gravells A & Simpson S (2008) *Planning and Enabling Learning in the Lifelong Learning Sector*. Exeter: Learning Matters.

Websites
Businessballs (2009): **www.businessballs.com**
Data Protection Act (1988): **www.opsi.gov.uk/Acts/Acts1998/ukpga_19980029_en_1**
Freedom of Information Act (2000): **www.opsi.gov.uk/Acts/acts2000/ukpga_20000036_en_1**
Guidance to Teachers and Employers, Literacy:
    www.dfes.gov.uk/curriculum_literacy/tree/writing/writingcomp/l2/
LLUK (Sept. 2008) Evidencing Personal Skills in Literacy and Numeracy: **www.lluk.org/**
    documents/evidencing-personal-skills-requirements.pdf
Minimum Core (2007): **www.lluk.org.uk/minimum_core_may_2007_3rd.pdf**
Plain English Campaign (2008): **www.plainenglish.co.uk/gobble.htm**
Qualifications and Curriculum Authority (2004) Communication Key Skill, QCA:
    www.qca.org.uk/14-19/11-16-schools/index_s5-3-using-key-skills.htm

Extracts from the Minimum Core Framework

Throughout this book you have been developing your understanding and skills relational to the Minimum Core requirements for literacy.

Part B of the Minimum Core Framework refers to Personal Language Skills (Literacy, pages 20–24). Extracts from this section are illustrated in the table below.

Speaking	Personal language skills for teaching and professional life. This requires trainee teachers to be able to:
Expressing yourself clearly, using communication techniques to help convey meaning and to enhance the delivery and accessibility of the message.	• express themselves clearly and use a range of communication techniques with a range of people for different purposes.
	• structure material; • use a logical sequence and make connections; • use verbal illustrations, analogy and real-life examples.
Demonstrating the ability to use language, style and tone in ways that suit the intended audience, and to recognise their use by others.	• use language style and tone appropriate to the audience; • recognise the use of language, style and tone of others. Appropriate use of language should include: • varying the level of formality according to audience and purpose; • adapting the delivery according to the level, needs and prior knowledge of the audience; • using pitch, pace, stress and intonation to convey and reinforce meaning; • explaining specialist terminology or jargon; • avoiding excessive or unnecessary use of idiomatic English. Identifying and recognising the language use of others should include: • identifying appropriate and inappropriate use of language by others; • recognising the motivation of others' language use; • evaluating the effectiveness of other speakers' language use.

Speaking	Personal language skills for teaching and professional life. This requires trainee teachers to be able to:
Using appropriate techniques to reinforce oral communication, to check how well the information is received and to support the understanding of those listening.	• reinforce oral communication; • check how well the information is received; • support the understanding of those listening.
	Trainee teachers should understand when a technique is being used to reinforce, check or support. Appropriate techniques should include: • repeating, rephrasing and summarising; • the provision of written notes or bullet pointed summaries; • the use of visual aids such as charts, diagrams and flowcharts; • employing a range of questioning techniques; • requesting feedback and responding appropriately; • asking for a summary of information given.
Using non-verbal communication to assist in conveying meaning and receiving information, and recognising its use by others.	This requires trainee teachers to be aware of how communication is affected and assisted by the use of non-verbal features. Awareness should include: • the use of a range of non-verbal communication to support, assist and refine; • the interpretation of the non-verbal signals of others; • the understanding that non-verbal features may convey different meanings in other cultures.
Listening	Personal language skills for teaching and professional life. This requires trainee teachers to be able to:
Listening attentively and responding sensitively to contributions made by others.	• use the linguistic and cultural conventions that demonstrate active listening and responding during discussions and oral exchanges; • use a range of listening skills, techniques and responses.

Listening	**Personal language skills for teaching and professional life.**
	Listening skills, techniques and responses should include: • listening face-to-face and via technology with individuals and groups; • listening for different purposes; • a range of non-verbal, confirmatory and questioning techniques to show active listening and response.
Reading	**Personal language skills for teaching and professional life.** **This requires trainee teachers to be able to:**
Find and select information from a range of reference material and sources of information, including the internet.	• access a wide range of information sources; • access relevant sources of information for different audiences. This requires trainee teachers to be aware of different approaches to conducting general and specific enquiries. Enquiry approaches should include the use of both paper-based and electronic systems.
Use and reflect on a range of reading strategies to interpret texts and to locate information or meaning.	**This requires trainee teachers to be able to:** • use different strategies for locating information within texts and for extracting meaning; • use strategies appropriate to the purpose for reading. Reading strategies should include: • skimming, scanning, detailed and critical reading. Reading should be undertaken for a range of purposes

Identify and record the key information or messages contained within reading material using note-taking techniques.	**This requires trainee teachers to be able to:** • identify key information or messages in a text; • record this information using note-taking techniques appropriate to both the purpose of and the audience for the notes. A range of techniques for identifying the key information, themes and concepts within a text should be included (e.g., annotation of the text or text-marking). A range of note-taking techniques should be included (e.g., linear and diagrammatic styles).
Writing	**Personal language skills for teaching and professional life.**
Write fluently, accurately and legibly on a range of topics.	Writing fluently should include: • implementing the various stages of the writing process; • structuring the content appropriately. Writing accurately should include: • ensuring that spelling, punctuation and use of grammar is accurate. Writing legibly should include: • using a printed or cursive style in handwritten documents that can be read easily; • using a font size and style appropriate to the intended audience in word-processed documents.
Select appropriate format and style of writing for different purposes and different readers.	Selection should include: • following the standard conventions for different text types; • following the standard conventions for texts with different functions; • demonstrating an awareness of the intended audience.
Use spelling and punctuation accurately in order to make meaning clear.	**This requires trainee teachers to be able to:** • use a range of checking mechanisms and understand their limitations. Checking mechanisms should include: • personal proofreading; • the use of dictionaries; • the use of electronic spell-checking devices.

	• use the full range of punctuation accurately; • use punctuation to establish meaning; • use punctuation according to accepted rules and conventions; • use punctuation to achieve specific effects.
Understand and use the conventions of grammar (the forms and structures of words, phrases, clauses, sentences and texts) consistently when producing written text.	**This requires trainee teachers to be able to:** • use grammar accurately in order to convey meaning; • use syntax according to accepted rules and conventions; • use grammar to achieve specific effects; • use grammar to achieve specific effects; • avoid common errors and confusions; • understand the appropriate meta-language.

Answers to key questions

Chapter 1: Communication

Q1 1. information
2. demonstration
3. telephone
4. as soon as possible
5. competition
6. typographical error

Q2 Consult a friend, colleague or tutor.

Q3 1. approval
2. disapproval
3. success
4. motivated
5. applause

Q4 You could use verbal or written communication for all of them.

Q5 When considering ethics and **confidentiality** it is important to remember the **Data Protection** Act and the **Freedom** of **Information Act** These two **acts** are to protect the public and that includes your learners.

Q6 Consult a friend, colleague or tutor.

Q7 Consult your dictionary.

Q8 • Use of slang – yea, doin, OK, hot.
• Too familiar when using Deborah's name – Debbie's, Deb's.
• Use of jargon – mocks, Moodle, refec, CATS, Uni.
• Use of filler – em.
• Info – information, exams – examinations.

Q9 Check your answers with a friend, colleague or tutor.

Q10 You should answer 'no' to all of these questions

Q11 Discuss your answers with a friend, colleague or tutor. This exercise should help identify which areas you need to work on.

Chapter 2: Reading

Q1 1. Further Education National Training Organisation
2. Further Education
3. Continuing Professional Development
4. Institute for Learning
5. Qualified Teacher Learning and Skills
6. Lifelong Learning UK

Q2 (c) The current standards are provided by LLUK.

Q3 1. Orr 2008
2. OFSTED 2003
3. March 2008
4. FENTO 2001
5. Equipping Our Teachers 2004
6. Foster Review 2004

Q4 (d) To meet the needs of a diverse workforce, regulations and reports were written to enable the FE workforce to become professionalised and regulated.

Q5 (c) Trainee teachers

Q6 Teaching, Lifelong Learning Sector, professional

Q7 1.(b) Not attributing information to the appropriate author.
2.(c) Frequency of gobbledygook.
3.(d) Searching for the gist from a piece of text.
4.(c) Looking for key words from within text.

Q8 Consult your dictionary.

Q9 Consult your thesaurus.

Q10 1. The Institute for Learning (IfL).
2. Five years.
3. DTLLS and also to meet the Minimum Core requirements.
4. At least 30 hours CPD annually.

Chapter 3: Writing conventions

Q1 *Hello Dave*

Would it be possible for me to swap a class at 3pm with Liz next Wednesday (14 March)? I can cover her class on the following Monday (19 March) at 3pm. I need to go to a professional development meeting on the Wednesday. The meeting is about behaviour management and I think the information could be very useful to me when I am teaching. Will you let me know as soon as possible please so that I can confirm or decline my attendance at the meeting?

Sue

Q2 Here is an example of how this paragraph could be condensed:

On Tuesday, 6 May, 2008, I witnessed six learners fighting outside RB3. I spoke to the learners and two of them informed me that they thought that two of the others had stolen money from them. I told them to go and see their course tutor and that I would be reporting the incident to the Head of Department.

Q3 Consult a friend, colleague or tutor.

Q4   Consult a friend, colleague or tutor.

Q5   Here is an example of a suitable letter:

SUBURBIA COLLEGE
Littlehaven Road
Sprigshire
SP11 2DM
Telephone 01234 567890, Facsimile 01234 567899

Confidential

FAO Mr L Tyler
The Garden Restaurant
20 Church Road
Little Lawton
Sprigshire
SP5 2JM

17 June 2008

Dear Mr Tyler

Re: Reference for Jason Ronald Hill

I have known Jason Hill for two years. He enrolled on a two-year A Level Business Studies programme in September 2006 and he is due to take his final examinations in a few weeks' time.

Jason has had an exemplary attendance record. He is also very good at time management and always hands his work in by the given deadlines.

I believe Jason to be an honest and trustworthy person. He communicates well with his peers and has been particularly supportive of one learner this year who has been absent from the college and has needed some peer support.

Throughout the two years Jason has engaged in extracurricular activities, specifically sports events and entrepreneurial activities. He recently received an award for designing a small business project.

I understand that the vacancy is for a Trainee Manager. I have no hesitation in recommending Jason for this position.

If you require further information please contact me.

Yours sincerely

Mr D McHin
Programme Leader, Business Studies

cc: Learner Service Department

Q6   Consult a friend, colleague or tutor.

Q7   Consult a friend, colleague or tutor.

Q8   1. No
       2. Yes
       3. No
       4. Yes

5. Yes
6. No
7. Yes
8. Yes
9. No
10. No

Q9 Register is the **style** that you would use to convey meaning; whereas syntax is the way you **construct** your sentences. Letters should always have a **salutation** and a **complimentary close**. Moreover a **date** and an **address** should always be included. A further point is that you should not use **colloquialisms** in formal correspondence. Finally it is important that you **proofread** your work before sending it to the recipient.

Q10 Neither nor; either or; should have; could have (never use *could/should of*).

Q11 Consult your dictionary.

Q12 (c) When sending a text via a mobile phone.

Q13 Dear Sir (or Dear Madam) – Yours faithfully

Dear Mrs Smith (or Dear Mr Smith) – Yours sincerely

Chapter 4: Punctuation

Q1 *This paper's purpose is to explore concepts and policies relating to the professionalism of Further Education (FE), also referred to as the Lifelong Learning sector, and the underpinning fundamental principles upon which the current and future initial teacher training (ITT) programmes within FE are, and should be, developed.*

The paper has been organised to combine relevant historical background of FE with current notions of what the fundamental principles are or should be within FE. Within this content, the objectives are to analyse and evaluate teacher training models and teaching cultures within FE. Also given importance within the assignment are differing theories of professionalism and some conflicting arguments relating to whether or not lecturers actually want to become professionalised.

Unless otherwise stated the term 'teacher' refers to working teaching staff within FE, as does the term 'lecturer'. Literature uses both of these terms to mean the same thing.

Q2 Two dots above each other are called a **colon** whereas a dot with a comma below it is called a **semi-colon**. If you want to break a sentence up without using a full stop you could use a **comma** or a pair of **brackets**. A **hyphen** joins two words together to make one different word. I think that I will scream if I see another **exclamation mark** at the end of a sentence where there should be a **question mark** or a **full stop**.

Q3
1. The cat's ball had burst.
2. The learners' work had been marked.
3. The door was coming off its hinge.
4. When I was teaching this afternoon I noticed that the children's chairs had been rearranged.
5. My work was at my sister's house.
6. It's a good thing that the learners arrived at their class on time.

7. All of the girls' mothers had attended the event.
8. The babies' bottles were all washed.
9. The baby's rattles were on the floor.
10. The learners' homework was handed in on time.

Q4 1. eyes
2. children's
3. greengrocers, carrots, son's

Q5 1. (b) a verb
2. (a) and
3. (b) for proper nouns

Q6 1. LLUK
2. i.e. or ie
3. e.g. or eg
4. PGCE or P.G.C.E.
5. D.I.U.S. or DIUS

Q7 Co-opt, co-operative, man-made, part-time, T-shirt, ante-natal, anti-war, pro-European

Q8 Can't, there's, who's, you're

Q9 Consult a friend, colleague or tutor.

Q10 1. Denry's theatre tickets.
2. The ladies' blue dresses.
3. The children's craft items.
4. The year's timetable.
5. The lecturers' equipment.

Chapter 5: Spelling

Q1 The following words are spelt incorrectly in the question. (Correct spellings provided here).

all right	bureaucracy	calendar	achieve
definitely	obsolete	curriculum	colleague
maintenance	quantitative	grammar	conscientious
sincerely		ordinary	liaise
temporarily		thorough	occurrence
withhold			separately
			synthesis
			xenophobia

Q2

Prefix	Root	Suffix
un	relate	ed
dis	joint	ed
mis	led	
dis	proportionate	
mis	fortune	
dis	honest	
	regard	ing
mis	behave	ing (no e)
	agree	ment
	use	ful

Q3
1. breaks
2. accommodation
3. Principal
4. already
5. cancelled
6. unfortunately
7. rigorous
8. advice
9. statements, supersede
10. off, thought, too

Q4 Questions:

1.(b) right
2.(a) to
3.(b) pair
4.(a) bored
5.(b) see

Q5 re-main-der   dis-cip-line
teach-er   suc-cess-ful
as-sign-ment   te-le-phone
class-room   tem-per-a-ture
re-source   ex-cel-lent

Q6 Consult your dictionary.

Q7 Consult your dictionary.

Q8
1. cotton
2. criteria
3. curricula
4. formulae or formulas
5. humans
6. injuries
7. lice
8. wheat

Q9 Consult your thesaurus.

Q10 Consult your dictionary.

Q11

Prefix		Suffix	
ante	before	able	of worth, capable of being
ex	finished	ish	being like something
mono	one	ed	changes the word to the past tense
anti	against	less	changes a word to form its opposite meaning
poly	more than one	ment	a condition or a result
hyper	very large	ness	a state or a quality

Chapter 6: Speaking and listening

Q1 Consult your thesaurus.

Q2
1. Associate Teacher Learning Skills
2. Certificate in Teaching in the Lifelong Learning Sector
3. Department for Industry, Universities and Schools
4. Diploma in Teaching in the Lifelong Learning Sector
5. Institute for Learning
6. Lifelong Learning UK
7. Not in Education, Employment or Training
8. Non-verbal Communication
9. Preparing to Teach in the Lifelong Learning Sector
10. Quality Improvement Agency
11. Qualified Teacher Learning and Skills
12. Special Educational Needs

Q3

	Idiom	Cliché	Colloquialism
Drop in the ocean	3		
Naff			3
Dab hand			3
Nest egg	3		
Stretch the truth		3	
Barbie			3
Actions speak louder than words	3		
As exciting as watching paint dry		3	
A piece of cake		3	
Billy no mates			3
Ivory tower		3	
Tickled pink	3		

Q4 Consult a friend, colleague or tutor.

Q5 *The experience was not new for all learners. The idea of considering where they stood in relation to other learners within the group was not new.*

Q6 Consult your dictionary and thesaurus.

Q7 1. Orally making a false statement about a person(s).
2. Forcefully/strongly deny the statement.
3. Somewhat guarded about it.
4. They are both cursed.
5. They were both cautioned.

Q8 1. me
2. me
3. she; me
4. He; them; us
5. Our

Glossary of terms

AB	Awarding Body
.ac	Academic
AL	Award Leader
ALI	Adult Learning Inspectorate
ATLS	Associate Teacher Learning and Skills
CATS	Credit Accumulation Transfer System
Cert.ed	Certificate of Education
CPD	Continuing Professional Development
CTLLS	Certificate in Teaching in the Lifelong Learning Sector
CV	Curriculum Vitae
DSCF	Department for Schools Children and Families
DfES	Department for Education and Skills
DIUS	Department for Industry, University and Skills
DPA	Data Protection Act
DTLLS	Diploma in Teaching in the Lifelong Learning Sector
EM	External Moderator
EMA	Educational Maintenance Allowance
ESOL	English Speakers of Other Languages
EV	External Verifier
FE	Further Education
FENTO	Further Education National Training Organisation
FOG	Frequency of Gobbledygook
FT	Full time
.gov	Government
HE	Higher Education
ICT	Information Communication Technology
IfL	Institute for Learning
ILP	Individual Learning Plan
ILT	Information Learning Technology
ISBN	International Standard Book Number
IT	Information Technology
ITT	Initial Teacher Training

IV	Internal Verifier
KISS	Keep it short and simple
LLUK	Lifelong Learning UK
LLS	Lifelong Learning Sector
NAB	National Awarding Body
NEET	Not in Education, Employment or Training
NTO	National Training Organisation
NVC	Non-verbal Communication
NVQ	National Vocational Qualifications
OFSTED	Office for Standards in Education
PCE	Professional Certificate in Education
PDP	Personal Development Plan
PGCE	Post Graduate Certificate in Education
PT	Part time
PTLLS	Preparing to Teach in the Lifelong Learning Sector
QAA	Quality Assurance Agency
QCA	Qualifications Curriculum Authority
QCF	Qualifications Credit Framework
QIA	Quality Improvement Agency
QTLS	Qualified Teacher Learning and Skills
Reflect	The IfL's online recording software to record CPD
SAR	Self-Assessment Report
SED	Self-Evaluation Document
SEN	Special Educational Needs
SENCO	Special Educational Needs Co-ordinator
SfL	Skills for Life, ESOL, Literacy, Mathematics
SMT	Senior Management Team
SMOG	Simple measure of gobbledygook
SVUK	Standards Verification UK
TEFL	Teaching English as a Foreign Language
TLQ	Tariff of Legacy Initial Teacher Training Qualifications
VAK	Visual Auditory Kinaesthetic
VLE	Virtual Learning Environment
www	World Wide Web

Index

abbreviations 45, 52
accents, as punctuation 44
accents, in speaking 8
accuracy 21, 28
acronyms 45, 52
active listening 71–2
active voice 67
acute accents (á) 44
Adult Core Curriculum
  communication 7
  punctuation 43
  reading 17
  speaking and listening 65
  spelling 56
  writing conventions 27
AIDA (attention, interest, desire, action) 34
'all ready'/'already', use of 60
'all right'/'alright', use of 60
ambiguity, and punctuation 51
ampersands (&)/'and', use of 44
analogies 69
'and'/ampersands (&), use of 44
annotating, in recording key information 22
'ante'/'anti', use of 60
apostrophes 49–51
appropriateness
  language use 10–11, 67, 68, 71
  reading material 21
  vocabulary 10, 68, 70
  see also audiences; readability
'as', in similes 69
Associate Teacher Learning and Skills
    (ATLS) status 1, 2
asterisks (*) 44
attention 65, 71, 73
audiences
  emails 30–1
  notices 33–4
  speaking 66, 67–9
  and writing styles 29, 30, 34
  see also appropriateness; formal
    communication; informal
    communication; jargon; readability;
    semi-formal communication
audio, use of 12
'auto', use of 58

backslashes (\) 44
bias, in reading material 21

body language see non-verbal
    communication
books 21–1
bracketing commas 47
brackets 47

'can', use of 35
capital letters 45
CD-ROMs 20
'cede'/'ceed'/'sede', use of 58
Certificate in Teaching in the Lifelong
    Learning Sector (CTLLS) 2
checking, of writing 19, 22, 28, 30, 38
citations 22, 33
clichés 68
coherence, of writing 30
cohesion, of grammar 37
colloquialisms 8, 32, 68, 71
colons 47
colour, and dyslexic learners 13
commas 44, 46, 51
communication
  Adult Core Curriculum 7
  cultural differences 8, 10, 12
  described 7
  errors 11–12, 30
  ethics and confidentiality 13
  hints and tips 10
  ICT (information communication
    technology) 12–13
  importance 7–8
  key questions 14–15
    answers 83
  legislation 13, 14, 33
  LLUK standards 7
  meta-language, appropriateness 10–11
  non-verbal communication 7, 8, 9,
    72, 73
  preparation 11, 67, 69
  presenting information 69–70
  see also errors; formal communication;
    informal communication; language
    use; listening; reading; semi-formal
    communication; speaking; writing
    conventions
'complement'/'compliment', use of 60
complimentary close conventions
  emails 31, 35

letters 32, 35
compound sentences 44, 46
concentration 66, 71, 73
conciseness, in writing 28, 35
confidentiality 13, 33
connective words and phrases 45, 46
consonants 56, 58
contexts, and writing style 29
continuing professional development
        (CPD) 13
contracted words 49
cultural differences 8, 10, 12
    see also teenage sub-cultures
currency, and information evaluation 21

dashes 48
Data Protection Act (1998) 14, 33
dialects 8
dictionaries 18, 57, 60
digital cameras 12
Diploma in Teaching in the Lifelong
        Learning Sector (DTLLS) status 1, 2
'dis', use of 57, 58
distractions 73
dividers 47
doodling 73
double consonants 58
drafting 27–8, 30
DVDs 12
dyslexia 13
    see also reading disabilities

'ed', use of 57
'e.g.', use of 52
'ei', use of 59
'either', use of 36
emails 12, 19, 30–1, 35
embedded functional skills 3
embedded literacy 3
ending conventions
    emails 31, 35
    letters 32, 35
errors
    mis-communication 11–12, 30
    writing conventions
        avoiding errors 35–8
        grammatical 11–12, 28, 34
        spelling mistakes 19, 28, 30, 34
        (*see also* checking, of writing;
            dictionaries; proofreading; spell
            checkers)
ethics 13
evidence, for Minimum Core 2–3
exclamation marks 46

eye contact 9, 72

facial expressions 9, 72
feedback, when listening 72
FENTO (Further Education National
        Training Organisation) standards 1
fonts 12, 34, 36
footnotes 44
formal communication
    emails 30, 31, 35
    grammar 37
    presentations 67
    reports 32–3
    and social learning and modelling 8
    writing styles 29
forms, writing 34
Freedom of Information Act (2000) 14, 33
Frequency of Gobbledygook (FOG) index
        20
full stops 46, 47

gestures 9, 72
glossaries of terms, provision 70, 71
glossary of terms (in this book) 91–2
gossip 14
grammar 35–8
    see also phrases; pronouns; sentences;
        verbs; words
grammatical errors 12, 28, 34
grave accents (à) 44
greeting conventions 31, 32

handouts 11
handwriting 22, 28, 34
hard copy, and information searching 21
Harvard referencing system 33
'has', use of 37
hashes (#) 44
'have', use of 35, 37
hearing impairments 13
hints and tips
    communication 10, 11
    listening 72, 73
    punctuation 46, 49, 51, 52
    reading 22
    speaking 66, 67, 69
    spelling 57, 59, 60
    writing conventions 29, 32, 36, 38
homophones 58, 59
hyphens 48

'I', use of 38, 46, 67
ICT (information communication
        technology) 12–13

see also CD-ROMs; emails; Internet;
    mobile phones; spell checkers; text
    messages; word-processing
idioms 68
'i.e.', use of 52
'ie'/'ei', use of 59
'ies'/'y', use of 58
images 12, 13
impressions 8, 27, 56
informal communication 8, 30, 31, 33, 67
information evaluation 21
information presentation 11, 67–71
information searching 18–19, 20–2
information sources 20–2
Information Technology (IT) technicians 13
Initial Teacher Training (ITT) 1
Institute for Learning (IfL) 1, 2
interactive whiteboards 12
interjections 65, 72, 73
Internet 12, 20–2, 44
interruptions 65, 72, 73
intonation 67, 69, 71
inverted commas 48
'is', in metaphors 69
'its'/'it's', use of 49

jargon 10–11, 35, 68, 71
    see also readability
joining commas 44, 46
journals 20, 21

key questions
    communication 14–16
        answers 83
    punctuation 52–4
        answers 86–7
    reading 23–5
        answers 83–4
    speaking and listening 74–5
        answers 89–90
    spelling 61–3
        answers 87–9
    writing conventions 38–41
        answers 84–6
keywords/key words 21, 22, 70

language and literacy Minimum Core
    component 70–80
language skills, self-audit 5–6
language use
    appropriateness 10–11, 67, 68, 71
    persuasive, in writing 29
    social learning and modelling 8

speaking 8,10–11, 67, 68, 71
languages, use of accents 44
learners with specific difficulties 13, 36
legibility, and note-taking 22
legislation 13, 14, 33
letter writing 31–2, 34
letters (alphabetic) 44, 45, 49
Licence to Practise 1
Lifelong Learning Sector (LLS), described 1
'like', in similes 69
listening
    active 71–2
    Adult Core Curriculum 65
    audiences 66
    barriers 73
    development of skills 65
    hints and tips 72, 73
    key questions 74–5
        answers 89–90
    LLUK (Lifelong Learning UK) standards 65
    Minimum Core 78–9
    passive 71
    and preparation for communication 11
    problems 66, 71–2
    purposes 66
    self audit 5 6
listing colons 47
listing commas 46
listing semi-colons 48
literacy skills, self-audit 5–6
LLUK (Lifelong Learning UK) 2–3
    see also LLUK (Lifelong Learning UK)
        standards; Minimum Core
LLUK (Lifelong Learning UK) standards
    communication 7
    described 1
    listening 65
    punctuation 43
    reading 17
    speaking 65
    spelling 56
    writing conventions 27
'ly', use of 57

magazines 20
'may', use of 35–6
'me', use of 38, 67
memory, and note-taking 22
meta-language, appropriateness 10–11
metaphors 68–69
Minimum Core 77–80
mirroring 72
'mis', use of 57, 58

mis-communication 12, 30
    see also checking, of writing;
        dictionaries; errors; grammatical
        errors; proofreading; spelling
        mistakes
mobile phones 13, 30
modelling, of communication 8, 71
monotones 66, 69
multiple sentences 44, 47

names, and capital letters 45
National Qualification Framework 1–2
negative communication 10, 11, 72, 73
'neither', use of 36
newspapers 20, 21
non-verbal communication 7, 8, 9, 71–2,
    73
'nor', use of 36
note-taking 11, 22, 73
notices, writing 33–4
nouns, homophones of verbs 59
numbers 51

obliques (/) 44
'of', use of 35
OFSTED 3, 12
'ology', use of 58
omission of letters 44, 49
omission of words 44, 46
online forms 34
'or', use of 36

pace *see* speed of reading; speed of
    speaking
paragraphs 29, 30, 45
paraphrasing, recording key information 22
parentheses 47
passive listening 71
passive voice 67
personal names, and capital letters 45
personal pronouns 37–8, 46, 67
Personal Skills 2
persuasive language, in writing 29
'phone', use of 58
phones, mobile 13, 30
phrases 30, 45, 46
    see also analogies; clichés;
        metaphors; similes
physical contact 10
pitch 67
place names, and capital letters 45
plagiarism 22
planning, of writing 27–8, 30
plural words 36, 37, 50–1

polysyllabic words 60
positive language 11
possessive pronouns 37
possessive use of apostrophes 50
posture 9, 72
preciseness, in writing 28, 35
prefixes 57, 58
preparation, for communication 11–12,
    67, 69
presenting information 11, 67–71
professional associations 1
Professional Formation 2
professionalism 13, 27, 56, 67
pronouns 37–8, 46, 67
pronunciation 44, 70
proofreading
    dictionaries 18, 57, 60
    emails 19, 30
    handouts and presentations 11
    hints and tips 22
    importance 19, 28
    notices 33–4
    spell checkers 19, 56, 60
proper nouns 45
punctuation
    abbreviations and acronyms 45, 52
    Adult Core Curriculum 43
    and ambiguity 51
    apostrophes 49
    brackets 47
    capital letters 45
    colons 47
    commas 44, 46–7, 51
    described 43
    exclamation marks 46
    full stops 46, 47
    hints and tips 46, 49, 51, 52
    hyphens and dashes 48
    importance 43
    key questions 52–4
        answers 86–7
    LLUK (Lifelong Learning UK) standards 43
    paragraphs 45
    question marks 46
    quotation marks/inverted
        commas/speech marks 45, 48–9
    semi-colons 48
    sentences 44, 47, 48

qualifications 1, 2–3
Qualified Teacher Learning and Skills
    (QTLS) 2
question marks 46
questioning 11, 70, 71, 72, 73
quotation marks 45, 48–9

re-reading, of writing 19, 22, 28, 30, 38
readability 19, 34
    see also jargon
reading
    Adult Core Curriculum 17
    hints and tips 22
    importance 17
    information sources and information
        searching 20–1
    key questions 23–5
        answers 83–4
    LLUK standards 17
    Minimum Core 79
    practice 17–18
    and preparation for communication 11
    proofreading (*see* proofreading)
    re-reading, of writing 11, 70, 71, 72, 73
    readability 19–20, 34
    recording key information 22
    self-audit 6
    speed 17
    strategies 18–19
reading aloud 18
reading disabilities 13, 18, 36
recapping, of speaking 70, 73
recording key information 11, 22, 73
referencing 22, 33
reflexive pronouns 37
register, and writing styles 29
relative pronouns 37
repetitiveness, in writing 28, 29
report writing 32–3
root words 57

salutation conventions 30, 31
scanning 18
search terms, for information searching 21
'sede'/'cede'/'ceed', use of 58
self-audit, of language and literacy skills
    5–6
semi-formal communication 31, 35, 68
semi-colons 48
sentences 37, 44, 47, 48, 67
signatures 32
similes 69
Simple Measure of Gobbledygook (SMOG)
    index 20
simple sentences 44
singular words 37, 50
skimming 18
slander 14
slang 8, 71
slashes (/) 44
social differences 8, 10, 13
social learning 8, 65

software 12–13
    see also spell checkers; word-
        processing
spatial awareness 10
speaking
    Adult Core Curriculum 65
    audiences 66, 67, 68–9
    described 7, 9
    development of skills 65
    hints and tips 66, 67, 69
    key questions 74–5
        answers 89–90
    language use 8, 10–11, 67, 68, 71
    LLUK (Lifelong Learning UK) standards 65
    and Minimum Core 77–8
    presenting information 67–71
    problems 66
    purposes 66
    recapping 73
    self-audit 5
    speed 67, 69
    thinking first 11, 66
    words, choosing 70
    see also questioning
speech marks 48, 49
speed of reading 17
speed of speaking 67, 69
spell checkers 19, 56–7, 60
spelling
    Adult Core Curriculum 56
    dictionaries 18, 57, 60
    double consonants 58
    hints and tips 57, 59, 60
    homophones 58, 59
    'ie'/'ei', use of 59
    importance 56
    key questions 61–3
        answers 87–9
    LLUK (Lifelong Learning UK) standards 56
    polysyllabic words 60
    proofreading (see proofreading)
    root words 57
    rules 60
    spell checkers 19, 56–7, 60
    vowels and consonants 56, 57, 58
spelling mistakes 19, 30, 34
    see also dictionaries; proofreading;
        spell checkers
statements, in sentences 44
'stationery'/'stationary', use of 60
'sub', use of 57
subjects, in sentences 37, 44, 67
suffixes 57
summarising 18, 22, 33

swearing 71
syllables 18
syntax 29

technical words 68–9
  see also jargon
teenage sub-cultures 8, 11, 69
tenses 37
terminology, glossary (of terms in this
      book) 89–90
terminology, provision of glossaries 71
text messages 30
'that', use of 36
'they're'/'their'/'there', use of 59
thinking, in preparation for speaking 11, 66
time, speaking 73
timeframes, and information searching 21,
      22
tone of voice 66, 67, 69, 71
training courses, for ICT (information
      communication technology) 13

unfamiliar words 70, 71

verbal communication *see* speaking
verbs 37, 44, 59
video clips 12
virtual learning environments (VLEs) 12
visual, audio and kinaesthetic (VAK)
      modes of learning 12, 13
visual impairment 13, 36
vocabulary
  appropriateness 10, 68, 70
  presenting spoken information 69, 70, 71
  and social learning 8
  and writing styles 29, 35
voice 66, 67, 69, 71
vowels 56, 57

'ware', use of 58
'which', use of 36

'whose'/'who's', use of 50
word-processing 30, 36
words 30, 70–1
  see also colloquialisms; connective
      words and phrases; contracted
      words; dictionaries; homophones;
      jargon; keywords/key words;
      omission of words; plural words;
      polysyllabic words; punctuation;
      root words; singular words; spell
      checkers; spelling; synonyms;
      technical words; unfamiliar words;
      vocabulary; word-processing
writing conventions
  Adult Core Curriculum 27
  coherence 30
  defined 7, 27
  emails 12, 19, 30–1, 35
  errors, avoiding 35–8
  forms 34
  hints and tips 29, 32, 36, 38
  importance 27, 32
  key questions 38–41
    answers 84–6
  letters 31–2, 34
  LLUK standards 27
  logical presentation 29
  Minimum Core 80
  notices 33–4
  planning and drafting 27–8, 30
  preciseness and conciseness 28, 35
  reports 32–3
  self-audit 6
  and social learning 8
  styles and formats for different purposes
      and audiences 29, 30, 34

'y'/'ies', use of 58
'your'/'you're', use of 50